1 MONTH OF FREE READING

at

www.ForgottenBooks.com

By purchasing this book you are eligible for one month membership to ForgottenBooks.com, giving you unlimited access to our entire collection of over 1,000,000 titles via our web site and mobile apps.

To claim your free month visit:

www.forgottenbooks.com/free1121906

ISBN 978-0-331-42356-3
PIBN 11121906

TOWN OF BELMONT.

LIST OF

Persons Assessed for a Poll Tax

AS OF

April 1, 1915.

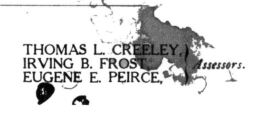

THOMAS L. CREELEY,
IRVING B. FROST,   *Assessors.*
EUGENE E. PEIRCE,

THE BELMONT PRESS
1915.

TOWN OF BELMONT.

LIST OF

Persons Assessed for a Poll Tax

AS OF

April 1, 1915.

THOMAS L. CREELEY,
IRVING B. FROST,   } *Assessors.*
EUGENE E. PEIRCE,

THE BELMONT PRESS
1915.

Assessed Polls - Belmont - 1915.

PRECINCT 1.

ALEXANDER AVENUE.

No.	Name.	Age.	Occupation.	Residence 1914
7	Slade, Harold L.	24	Market gardener	same
	Grillo, John	31	Barber	"
	Yantosca, Murray	26	Chauffeur	Somerville
123	Morrisey, John J.	52	Farmer	same
123	Gilpatrick, Charles	50	"	"
159	McCarthy, John F.	23	Plumber	"
	Comeau, Frank	48	Carpenter	
52	Kenrick, Bowman H.	62	Manager	
52	Kenrick, Oscar B.	26	Farmer	
52	Kenrick, Walter H.	28	Chauffeur	

ASH STREET.

No.	Name.	Age.	Occupation.	Residence 1914
7	Chamian, G. H.	26	Carpet repairer	same
7	Alexander, Alec	36	" "	"
9	Morrow, James L.	20	Clerk	"
9	Morrow, William J.	22	Mechanic	
9	Morrow, William W.	54	Shipper	
11	Jefferson, John R.	57	Farm hand	
11	Sliney, Thomas	43	Laborer	
13	Hanson, Michael	69	Carpenter	
15	Taylor, James H.	25	Mechanic	
17	Sliney, Michael	40	Laborer	
19	Maguire, John F.	30	Teamster	

BAKER STREET.

No.	Name.	Age.	Occupation.	Residence 1914
15	Narbut, Walter S.	42	Manufacturer	same
17	Craven, William	26	Postal clerk	"
17	Sweeney, Maurice H.	48	Contractor	"
23	Newman, Philip	69	Laborer	
25	Ryan, Thomas	50	Teamster	
29	Spegio, Frank	50	"	"
39	Otiro, Harry	24	Barber	Waverley
39	Perino, Harry	22	"	same
39	Mufficci, Michael	40	Laborer	"
55	Zona, John	30	Piano finisher	East Boston
57	Pitrone, Angelo	20	Carpenter	R. I.
57	Bruno, Rocco	36	Piano finisher	same
59	Valenti, Tony	25	Candy maker	East Boston
59	Nazzaro, Joseph	38	Foreman	" "
	Swaduski, Jake	35	Brick maker	Trowbridge st.
54	Ricco, Antonio	32	Machinist	same
40	Convineu, Frank	54	Laborer	"
40	Hernesz, Lovatti	26	"	"

BAKER STREET, - Continued.

No.	Name.	Age.	Occupation.	Residence 1914.
	Kessler, William	30	Teamster	Penn.
	Burke, William H.	55	Merchant	same
12	Perino, Nicola	30	Farm hand	"
12	Galgano, Joseph	54	Laborer	"

BLAKE STREET.

	Scott, Frank A.	35	Teacher	same
	Hayes, Lloyd B.	35	Secretary	Cambridge
14	Finlay, Chas. W.	50	Jeweller	East Boston
12	Tucker, George M.	53	Advertising Agent	80 Goden St.

BRIGHT ROAD.

	Dana, Edward	29	Ass't Supt.	same

BRIGHTON STREET.

No.	Name.	Age.	Occupation.	Residence 1914.
31	Griffin, William	37	Farm hand	same
31	Riley, Patrick	30	" "	"
31	Loftus, John	27	Clerk	"
31	Loftus, James F.	25	Farm hand	
159	Weston, George M.	71	Night Watchman	
159	Weston, Willis P.	36	Gardener	
319	Staples, Warren	20	Farm hand	"
319	Staples, John L.	49	" "	
321	McKenn, Henry	34	Bottler	308 Brighton St.
310	Lee, Alphonse	42	Brickmaker	same
308	Zelefiski, Tony	28	" "	Trowbridge St.
300	Keenan, James A.	50	Station agent	same
300	Keenan, Francis R.	26	Salesman	"
244	Plunkett, William	31	"	"
244	Plunkett, Richard	36	Engineer	
244	Cheshire, George	55	Retired	
152	Dixon, George	62	Foreman	
122	Harris, Fred B.	25	Farmer	
122	Stearns, Edward H.	48	"	
102	Kenny, Michael	27	Farm hand	
102	Tilton, William	23	Farmer	
102	Ryan, John W.	27	"	
44	Bresnan, Cornelius F.	20	Salesman	
44	Bresnan, Cornelius J.	55	Farmer	
26	Parks, Edward A.	28	Conductor	
26	Parks, Fred H.	63	Coachman	

CEDAR ROAD

No.	Name.	Age.	Occupation.	Residence 1914
27	Purrington, Oliver	35	Clergyman	New Bedford
35	Husband, Alexander P.	22	Salesman	same
35	Husband, John	27	Builder	"
35	Husband, Robert G.	51	"	"
26	Stone, Howard A.	49	Salesman	
	Chaffee, Emory F.	59	Real estate	

CENTER AVENUE.

No.	Name.	Age.	Occupation.	Residence 1914
23	Hatch, Simon D., Sr.	85	Retired	same
25	Hatch, Alvah J.	20	Clerk	"
25	Hatch, Ernest L.	23	Houseman	23 Center Ave.
25	Hatch, Simon D.	22	Plumber	same
25	Hatch, Alvah L.	50	Carpenter	"
	Norton, Arthur	34	Instructor	"
46	Jenney, Charles	40	"	
34	Fitzpatrick, Frank A.	63	Publisher	
26	O'Brien, John	55	Fireman	
26	O'Brien, Joseph F.	25	"	
26	O'Brien, John E.	26	Salesman	
26	O'Brien, William	23	Driver	

CHENERY TERRACE.

No.	Name.	Age.	Occupation.	Residence 1914
9	Brown, Frank W.	48	Manager	same
	Tierney, Nicholas W.	50	Hotel watchman	"
12	Bowler, William	43	Driver	"
2	La Bonte, Frank N.	40	Druggist	

CHERRY STREET.

No.	Name.	Age.	Occupation.	Residence 1914
10	Betford, Alfred E.	54	Salesman	same
10	Comeau, Louis	39	Carpenter	"
8	Prentice, Theodore J.	69	Letter carrier	"
8	Flett, W. Leonard	30	Chauffeur	
2	Belleveau, Edward	27	Carpenter	
2	Murphy, Daniel L.	31	Electrician	
2	Bourneuf, William	23	Carpenter	
2	Bourneuf, Leander F.	55	Carpenter	

CLARK STREET.

No.	Name.	Age.	Occupation.	Residence 1914
47	Kendall, Francis H.	44	Civil engineer	same
59	Dodge, Frederic	68	Judge U. S. Dist. Ct.	"
80	Sargent, James K. P.	69	Janitor	"

CLARK STREET, - Continued.

No.	Name.	Age.	Occupation.	Residence 1914.
80	Sargent, Frank F.	32	Salesman	same
70	Gano, Seth T.	35	Secretary and Treasurer	"
60	Watson, Rev. Charles H.	68	Clergyman	"
44	Colburn, Charles E.	75	Retired	
44	Ellison, Frank D.	48	Merchant	
	Putnam, Walter A.	45	"	

CLIFTON STREET.

No.	Name.	Age.	Occupation.	Residence 1914.
95	Brown, Harold I.	31	Teacher	Old Concord rd.
86	Davis, Daniel L.	24	Student	same
86	Davis, George W.	36	Clerk	"
86	Davis, Herbert E.	34	"	"

CLOVER STREET.

No.	Name.	Age.	Occupation.	Residence 1914.
1	Armstrong, George P.	58	Supt. of Schools	same
15	Cole, James T.	33	Superintendent	"
21	Stone, Joseph E.	36	Manager	"
27	Sherman, Herbert L.	31	Chemist	
35	Frenning, John E.	51	Manufacturer	
30	Stevens, Hermon W.	51	Advertising agent	
24	Kelso, Robert W.	34	Secretary	

COMMON STREET.

No.	Name.	Age.	Occupation.	Residence 1914.
25	Kendall, John H.	64	Retired	same
25	Kendall, Arthur S.	22	Student	"
25	Kendall, Francis H.	28	Real Estate	"
25	Kendall, Paul	20	Student	
45	Brown, Winthrop Jr.	22	Clerk	
45	Brown, Winthrop	52	Broker	
45	Brown, James	24	Salesman	
59	Hough, Charles G.	59	Weigher and gauger	"
211	Sands, Frank	70	Retired	"
211	Washburn, Dexter	52	Merchant	
233	Hoyt, Henry A.	80	Retired	
233	Rose, Joseph	67	Laborer	
268	Preston, Frank S.	50	Collector of Curios	"
216	Hittinger, Jacob	55	Retired	
200	Kelly, Herbert L.	56	Retired	
194	Houghton, Frank G.	47	"	
140	Carney, William	49	Farmer	
136	Penney, Nicholas J.	54	"	
130	Ryan, Jerry F.	56	Chief of Police	
130	Ryan, Lawrence M.	34	Meat Cutter	

COMMON STREET, - Continued.

No.	Name.	Age.	Occupation.	Residence 1914.
130	Ryan, Michael J.	59	Stableman	same
130	Ryan, Joseph J.	30	Foreman	"
116	Baxter, Rev. James J.	44	Clergyman	"
116	Dolan, Rev. Gerald L.	27	"	
100	Underwood, Henry O.	57	Merchant	
90	Underwood, Loring	40	Landscape architect	"
50	Underwood, Wm. J.	22	Student	..
50	Underwood, W. Lyman	51	Professor	

CONCORD AVENUE.

No.	Name.	Age.	Occupation.	Residence 1914.
5	Hopkins, Raymond A.	29	Electrical Engineer	Cambridge
5	Page, Maurice J.	31	Architect	same
5	Bonney, Robert D.	22	Chemist	Wakefield
7	Carlson, Emil	24	Painter	Cambridge
7	Knirsch, John	34	Machinist	same
17	Beck, Carl O.	26	Cabinet maker	Cambridge
17	Benson Gustaf	36	Painter	same
19	Peterson, Albert	30	Carpenter	"
19	Johnson, Julius E.	35	Brick layer	Cambridge
19	White, Patrick	61	Retired	Boston
19	Morette, Lawrence	31	Foreman	"
35	Anderson, H. Samuel	33	Instructor	same
35	McPartland, James	27	Machinist	Allston
35	Johnson, Axel	32	Cabinet maker	Cambridge
43	McDonald, Daniel	38	Painter	same
43	Eagan, John J.	41	Blacksmith	"
67	Arena, Joseph	50	Grocer	Boston
67	Arena, Harry	26	"	same
81	Reed, Leslie B.	23	Bookbinder	"
81	McCaig, Joseph	28	Clerk	"
81	McCaig, Robert E.	26	"	
85	Dill, Joseph H.	60	Mariner	
85	Dill, George N.	26	Clerk	
85	Metcalf, Raymond	27	Driver	
85	Metcalf, Frederick C.	29	Printer	
105	Drolette, Joseph	50	Laborer	
109	Bradett, Baptiste	44	Brick maker	
109	Boissoneau, Eugene	39	Laborer	
293	McGinnis, Patrick H.	55	Farmer	
293	McGinnis, Charles J.	62	Merchant	
293	McGinnis, Andrew	66	Retired	
319	Sliney, David	45	Janitor	
321	O'Toole, Peter	30	Gardener	
321	Collins, Patrick	35	Laborer	"
331	Millett, John	50	Teamster	25 Thomas st.
333	Millett, Patrick	43	Laborer	same
335	Morrisey, John J. Jr.	29	Laborer	"
335	Morrisey, John J. Sr.	50	"	"

CONCORD AVENUE, - Continued.

No.	Name.	Age.	Occupation.	Residence 1914.
337	Rogers, Joseph	28	Baggage master	same
371	White, Herbert	38	Laborer	101 Washington st.
371	Brennan, Patrick	48	"	7 Underwood st.
371	Sellers, William A.	27	Clerk	101 Beech st.
371	Sellers, Arthur	53	Janitor	" " "
385	Dunsford, Isaac	45	Livery	same
385	Ericson, Oscar	37	Driver	"
401	Parker, Horace	47	Station agent	"
527	Elson, Alfred W.	55	Publisher	
	Parker, Torrance	43	Lawyer	
	Southard, Charles B.	63	"	
	Kerrigan, John	31	Chauffeur	"
653	Mahoney, Daniel J.	44	Barber	Plymouth
Off	Fleming, John	30	Farmer	· same
741	Thomas, Charles R.	25	Teamster	"
741	Thomas, David L.	54	Contractor	"
682	Garland, James B.	58	Janitor	
682	Garland, Herbert	22	Clerk	
670	Ryan, Dennis	74	Farmer	
670	Ryan, Edward J.	35	"	
	Clark, John	50	"	
	Gardner, John	80	"	
Off	Jones, Charles L.	46	Manager	
"	Leahy, Martin W.	28	Laborer	
"	Meisel, Fred. J.	48	Lithographer	
	Meisel, Edward J.	46	"	
580	Atkins, Edwin F., Jr.	23	Student	"
580	Atkins, Edwin F.	66	Merchant	
560	Swain, Leonard	24	Student	Conn.
560	Swain, Edward	53	Retired	"
480	Burns, John A.	25	Teamster	63 Hull St.
480	McCarthy, Edmund	36	Fireman	same
480	Dowd, William	59	Laborer	"
392	McNeil, Prescott	20	Reporter	"
392	McNeil, John	61	Chauffeur	
392	Hands, James	58	Gardener	
Off	Wellington, C. Oliver	26	Accountant	
296	Mead, John H.	26	Policeman	
296	Mead, P. Henry	48	"	
184	Bump, Henry M.	44	Leather inspector	
184	Bump, Albert H.	20	Student	
184	Whelan, James F.	28	Grocer	
182	Robertson, Murdick	38	Gardener	
Off	Murphy, William	57	"	
	Chant, Frank D.	79	Supt. of streets	

COTTAGE STREET.

46	Shenan, Thomas	73	Laborer	same

COTTAGE STREET, - Continued.

No.	Name.	Age.	Occupation.	Residence 1914.
46	McDermott, Timothy F.	40	Teamster	same
42	O'Grady, Martin	75	Gardener	"
42	Sanderson, George J.	37	Watchmaker	"
38	Logan, Crayton	58	Watchman	
34	Greenwood, George W.	41	Machinist	
14	Ford, Thomas	40	Teamster	
12	McNeil, John E.	53	Painter	

CROSS STREET.

No.	Name.	Age.	Occupation.	Residence 1914.
35	Sullivan, Daniel	53	Farm hand	Lake st.
35	Spinna, Joseph	42	" "	same
85	Igo, William A.	25	Farmer	"
85	Igo, Bernard F.	39	"	"
85	Igo, Peter	66	"	
76	Thyne, John	50		
76	Cassidy, James	25		
76	Kylie, Morris	30		
76	Fleming, Richard	20		
76	Caserly, James	25		"
76	Crowley, Simon	33		Pleasant st.
76	Redding, Michael	25	"	"
76	Redding, Patrick	22	"	"
26	Hurley, Patrick T.	32	Salesman	same
26	Hurley, John H.	43	Farm hand	"
26	Hurley, Patrick	68	Farmer	"
24	Wall, William	49	Teamster	
24	Brosnahan, Thomas P.	38	Station agent	
24	Millerick, Patrick	30	Laborer	"
24	Burnick, Patrick	32	"	47 Thomas st.
20	Buckley, Daniel	35	Farm hand	same
20	Donovan, Timothy	54	" "	"
20	Hurley, William J.	22	Civil Engineer	"
20	Hurley, Patrick C.	52	Farm hand	
18	Hurley, John	48	Farmer	
16	Keefe, Michael	48	"	"
14	Shible, Albert	45	Carriage trimmer	Readville

FAIRMONT STREET.

No.	Name.	Age.	Occupation.	Residence 1914.
49	Runey, Leon C.	21	Student	same
56	Birch, Clifford W.	22	"	"
56	Birch, Harold W.	24	Manufacturer	"
56	Birch, Albert	50	"	

GODEN STREET.

No.	Name.	Age.	Occupation.	Residence 1914.
9	Sandiford, Ernest	50	Salesman	same

GODEN STREET, - Continued.

No.	Name.	Age.	Occupation.	Residence 1914.
9	Sandiford, Chester L.	21	Student	same
21	Jones, Walter F.	33	Printer	"
27	Gibb, Thomas R. P.	34	Lawyer	"
33	Mason, Theodore	60	Salesman	
33	Mason, Ralph	30	"	"
37	O'Neill, Joseph S.	38	Lawyer	Everett
67	Palmer, Benedict F.	66	Fish dealer	same
67	Palmer, Matthew J.	63	Retired	"
	Donahoe, John	50	Farmer	"
84	Taft, Roger B.	27	Dentist	Watertown
82	Chaffee, E. Leon	29	Instructor	Cambridge
74	Cannon, Willard S.	29	Salesman	same
74	Cannon, Winthrop D.	35	"	"
72	Nobriga, Charles B.	56	Architect and builder	"
64	Stearns, Milton S.	21	Student	Waltham
34	Robinson, Sumner B.	52	Manager	same
34	Robinson, Guy H.	24	Bookkeeper	"
30	Fenwick, Frank A.	20	Clerk	"
30	Fenwick, Ernest I.	53	Salesman	"
41	Robinson, Edgar W.	41	Manager	"
12	Cain, George H.	45	Instructor	4 Goden st.
4	Cox, Michael H.	37	Commission merchant	" "
4	Scanlon, Harold V.	21	Clerk	Everett

HEUSTIS

	Heustis, Lancaster H.	30	Inspector	same
	Heustis, Warren H.	55	Landscape gardener	"
	Campbell, Henry	57	Carpenter	Somerville

HILL ROAD.

	Miller, George H.	45	Piano maker	same
	Williams, Bertrand P.	26	Chauffeur	"
	Williams, Ralph E.	24	Piano regulator	"
	Hill, Amos E.	61	Farmer	68 Leonard st.
	Richardson, J. Herbert	67	Retired	" "

Dewey, Percy
Gardiner, Raynor

HOW

Locke, Richard B.
Barton, Charles A.

HURON AVENUE.

No.	Name.	Age.	Occupation.	Residence 1914.
26	Irving, Samuel R.	48	Stablekeeper	same
	Mannix, Timothy J.	32	Conductor	"
	Walker, James	65	Farm hand	"
	O'Connell, John	54	Watchman	Cambridge
	Richardson, J. Howard	62	Market gardener	same

KILBURN ROAD.

	Chase, Charles H.	60	Distiller	same
	Boynton, George H.	32	Bookkeeper	"
	Hammer, Chas. D.	71	Insurance	"
	Shaplaigh, William P.	24	Clerk	
	Kurtz, Charles C.	87	Accountant	
	Robinson, Edward K.	32	Editor	
	Sexton, George A.	32	Manager	

LAKE STREET.

354	Taylor, Arthur	50	Farmer	same
340	Hoar, Maurice	37	"	"
340	Scott, Charles O.	22	"	"
340	Costine, James	27	Salesman	
308	Frost, Sylvester C.	73	Farmer	
218	Freeman, Carl	49	Gardener	
218	McPhail, Murdock	47	Teamster	

LEONARD STREET.

15	Dacey, James	45	Farmer	same
17	Harty, William	53	Steamfitter	"
17	Harty, John F.	22	Salesman	101 Beech st.
27	Kennedy, John J.	26	Meat cutter	85 Beech st.
67	Locke, William I.	37	Farmer	same
113	Allyn, S. Bradford	32	Paying teller	"
68	Small, Dr. Ernest W.	35	Physician	628 Pleasant st.
68	Peirce, Eugene E.	47	Civil engineer	same
66	Callahan, William A.	35	Merchant	"
66	Webber, Arthur M.	25	Salesman	Off Concord ave.
64	Bacon, George H.	62	Mason	same
64	Bacon, Henry A.	34	"	"
38	Bellantoni, John	30	Fruit dealer	"
38	Depasquali, Tony	25	Barber	East Boston
34	Perault, Peter P.	37	Painter	same
34	Perault, Arthur L.	24	Salesman	"
34	Perault, John B.	69	Painter	"

MOORE STREET.

No.	Name.	Age.	Occupation.	Residence 1914
20	Sayles, Dwight M.	46	Bookeeper	same
18	Suydam, Charles	44	Postal office clerk	"
12	Jacobs, Percival D.	24	Salesman	California

MYRTLE AVENUE.

11	Finn, John V.	42	Supt. Shipping Dept.	same
17	Wilcock, John	41	Buyer	"
23	Crocker, Philander R.	42	Salesman	"
29	Elliott, James E.	60	Superintendent	
35	Wood, Henry B.	60	Civil engineer	
26	Moulton, David J.	54	Trav. salesman	
22	Wood, Dana M.	31	Civil engineer	
16	Sherman, Charles W.	44	" "	
10	Payne, Edward F.	44	Artist	

OAK STREET

11	Cate, Eleazar	50	Manufacturer	same
23	Woodin, George R.	55	Mining	"
29	Bathrick, John J.	45	Merchant	"
35	Maguire, Patrick	87	Retired	
41	Mason, J. Munroe	81	"	
42	Robbins, Arthur G.	53	Instructor	"
30	Jordan, Everard W.	52	Trav. salesman	112 School st.
30	Jordan, Raymond W.	21	Cutter	" "
24	Tuttle, Henry E.	58	Salesman	same
20	Worcester, Edwin G.	40	Merchant	"
14	Dudley, Warren P.	60	Secretary	"
8	Beaton, Herbert L.	24	Clerk	20 Marion rd.
8	Beaton, Peter A.	46	Plumber	" "
4	O'Hara, James W.	40	Postal clerk	11 Sunnyside pl.

OLD CONCORD ROAD.

	Kennedy, William S.	64	Writer	same

ORCHARD STREET.

	Rogers, Dr. Mark H.	37	Physician	Allston
61	Rollins, William S.	55	Moving picture owner	same
67	Brodrick, Royal T.	46	Town Treasurer	"
71	Read, Elmer C.	41	Merchant	"
	Ransom, Horace U.	29	Civil engineer	
	Morrison, James H.	37	Agent	

ORCHARD STREET, - Continued.

Occupation.

	Temple, Edward H., Jr.	30	Concrete engineer	same
	Colliers, Frank L.	34	Manager	..
	Morse, C. Harry	45	Clerk	
	Dunning, Geo. H.	62	Marketman	
	Morrison, Richard E.	27	Clerk	
	Howard, Francis J.	67	Insurance	
30	Furniss, William E.	40	Treasurer	"
24	Jones, St. Clair	35	Electrical engineer	Cambridge
	Robinson, Jabez L.	60	Metal worker	"."

ORCHARD STREET EXTENSION.

| | Orsett, Coy | 32 | Florist | Cambridge |

PLEASANT STREET.

289	Frost, Henry	83	Retired	same
301	Frost, Charles A.	72	"	"
307	Frost, Albert H.	31	Market gardener	"
343	Woods, Henry W.	65	Merchant	
)ff	Mead, John H.	22	Teamster	
)ff	Scarfo, Tony	35	Laborer	
)ff	Daley, Patrick	40	"	
)ff	Horn, Alvin H.	35	Teamster	"
)ff	Mead; Michael	45	Collector	352 Pleasant st.
439	Fletcher, Arthur	27	Farmer	same
439	Fletcher, J. Henry	70	Marketman	"
439	Eigenfeldt, John	34	Chauffeur	"
439	Howden, Charles	30	Gardener	"
467	Cleland, Fred E.	38	Printer	Somerville
483	Fletcher, Geo. V.	73	Marketman	same
519	Clark, Herbert A.	65	Salesman	"
561	Locke, William H.	25	Clerk	"
561	Locke, Isaac H.	64	Commission merchant	"
561	Locke, Isaac B.	31	".' "	
575	Locke, James E.	70	Farmer	
593	Brown, John H.	44	Carpenter	
593	Brown, William S.	21	"	
605	Cutler, Wolcott	24	Student	
605	Cutler, Wm. J.	50	Insurance	
613	Stone, Arthur P.	45	Lawyer	
631	Locke, George W.	80	Retired	
631	Wellington, Wm. W.	26	Student	
641.	Waldon, Charles H.	50	Shoe merchant	
671	Price, Lewis V.	72	Real estate	
701	Reed, Thomas E.	35	Salesman	
701	Reed, X. Allen	66	Express messenger	..
721	Hunt, Chandler R.	38	Insurance agent	

PLEASANT STREET, - Continued.

No.	Name.	Age.	Occupation.	Residence 1914
727	Robbins, Samuel D.	27	Teacher	same
727	Robbins, Chandler	58	Manufacturer	"
Off	Maguire, Patrick	39	Clerk	"
Off	Maguire, Edward	24	Plumber	
Off	Whalen, William	37	Motorman	
Off	Sullivan, William	22	Chauffeur	"
806	Berenson, Louis	39	Shoemaker	Lawrence
710	Cashman, Patrick	58	Janitor	same
642	Hapgood, Richard	74	Retired	"
634	Locke, George T.	36	Market gardener	"
626	Peirce, Owen M.	46	Salesman	
624	Jack, Horatio	42	"	
618	McDonald, Wm. W.	22	Expressman	
618	McDonald, William	51	"	
592	Abbot, E. Stanley	52	Physician	"
582	Stevens, Geo. W.	60	Retired	Boston
582	Lahty, Enoch Irving	25	Buyer	Oak st.
568	Baldwin, Harry H.	57	Merchant	same
568	Baldwin, Harry, Jr.	32	Clerk	"
560	Farnham, Edwin E.	46	Metal dealer	"
548	Sargent, Geo. M. D.	69	Market gardener	
536	Howe, Dr. Percy R.	50	Dentist	
536	Howe, James A.	80	Retired	
536	Howe, James A.	22	Cotton broker	
Off	Baker, Arthur A.	47	Laborer	
500	Walcott, George P.	71	Merchant	
490	Pound, Roscoe	54	Instructor	"
480	Frost, J. Fred	56	Retired	467 Pleasant st.
400	Hill, J. Willard	74	"	same
400	Hill, Alfred C.	27	Oil merchant	"
400	Hill, Willard M.	40	Fish dealer	"
400	Hill, Clarence O.	45	Bank clerk	"
352	Huston, Charles E.	32	Plasterer	Oxford av., Camb.
352	Russell, Geo. H.	83	Storekeeper	same
334	Price, Eden	70	Carriage manufacturer	"
334	Fisher, Harry P.	27	Milk driver	Franklin
330	Cushman, Geo. M.	33	Salesman	same
328	Chick, Harry W.	28	Cabinet maker	"
312	Frost, Walter L.	55	Market gardener	"
312	Frost, Walter E.	21	" "	
306	Frost, Irving B.	53	" "	
280	Frost, Everett A.	56	" "	

PROSPECT STREET.

	Name	Age	Occupation	Residence
	Coe, Rev. Reginald H.	60	Clergyman	same
	Freman, Hiram	23	Milk driver	"
	Henry, J. Wilbert	47	Milkman	"
	Crocker, Charles	47	Foreman	

PROSPECT STREET, - Continued.

No.	Name.	Age.	Occupation.	Residence 1914.
	Prentiss, George A.	66	Market gardener	"
	Prentiss, John H.	24	Civil engineer	
	Prentiss, Joseph	22	Student	

SCHOOL STREET.

No.	Name.	Age.	Occupation.	Residence 1914.
7	Shean, Patrick H.	35	Undertaker	same
27	McGlue, Hugh P.	53	Coachman	"
27	Merrill, Fletcher D.	70	Decorator	"
47	Reed, William J.	60	Meat cutter	"
53	Pressey, Edwin S.	58	Clergyman	Orange
53	Pressey, Sidney L.	26	Student	"
63	Parks, Frank E.	56	Janitor	same
83	Secor, Henry B.	45	Salesman	"
83	Austin, George	68	Painter	"
87	Bennett, James J.	48	Salesman	
93	Smith, George E.	57	Osteopath	
97	Sweat, Augustus T.	56	Merchant	
111	Moriarty, Oscar F.	54	"	
117	Taylor, Amos L.	38	Lawyer	
123	Beede, Everett Jefts	30	Manager	
	Cronin, Wm. P.	40	Merchant	
	Keville, William J.	37	Real estate	
	Chandler, Oscar M.	58	Chief clerk	"
104	Stearns, E. Truman	28	Salesman	Cambridge
90	Wilson, George L.	43	Lawyer	same
74	Tobin, Patrick F.	57	Marketman	"
70	Lockhart, Alexander C.	29	Bookkeeper	same
70	Stone, Joseph C. R.	28	Salesman	Wakefield
54	Grimes, William F.	56	Cloth examiner	same
54	Grimes, William F., Jr.	27	Draughtsman	"
54	Grimes, Arthur G.	24	Steamfitter	"
54	Grimes, J. Henry	21	Electrician	
50	McNaught, Arthur J.	48	Janitor	

SHEAN ROAD.

No.	Name.	Age.	Occupation.	Residence 1914.
	Shean, Patrick T.	68	Retired	same
	Shean, Patrick T., Jr.	38	Clerk	"

SOMERSET STREET.

No.	Name.	Age.	Occupation.	Residence 1914.
25	Locke, Edwin A.	25	Student	same
25	Locke, John A.	51	Painter	"
37	Simonds, James O.	48	Merchant	"
37	Simonds, Sidney L.	22	Student	
97	White, Clarence Scott	42	Artist	

SOMERSET STREET, - Continued.

No.	Name.	Age.	Occupation.	Residence 1914.
90	Reed, Andrew F.	68	Insurance	same
90	Woodberry, Robert C.	41	Artist	"
90	Emily, Harold	34	"	"
70	Arenstrop, Henry F.	74	Gardener	"
70	Sweetman, John	40	Laborer	480 Concord ave.
70	Drisken, Roger	29	"	Waverley
30	Simonds, James Otis	84	Merchant	same

SPINNEY TERRACE.

No.	Name.	Age.	Occupation.	Residence 1914.
1	Lunsford, Maurice P.	28	Salesman	Watertown
3	Palmer, Louis	30	Advert. manager	Cambridge
5	Dunbar, Harold C.	35	Artist	90 Somerset st.

SPRING STREET.

No.	Name.	Age.	Occupation.	Residence 1914.
140	Morton, Alfred M.	47	Farmer	same
78	Gass, James S.	45	Farm hand	"
78	Malone, Frank	40	Foreman	"
66	Ryan, Daniel	45	Farm hand	
66	Millerick, John	32	" "	
66	Ryan, Dennis	54	" "	"
16	Reilly, Matthew	29		Arlington
16	Reilly, Edward	58		same

STONE ROAD.

No.	Name.	Age.	Occupation.	Residence 1914.
1	McLean, Arthur W.	32	Lawyer	Cambridge
15	Sawyer, Fred S.	41	Draughtsman	Wakefield
	Green, Albert R.	44		Boston
	MacDonald, Albert J.	24	Architect	Hingham
	MacDonald, John	21	Salesman	"
94	Flint, Lester E.	33	Treasurer	same
	Brock, Ralph L.	31	Laundryman	Boston
24	Walker, Lyman W.	37	Farmer	Roslindale
	Hoyt, Samuel W.	35	Teacher	same

SUNNYSIDE PLACE.

No.	Name.	Age.	Occupation.	Residence 1914.
5	Adams, William L.	53	Retired	same
7	O'Brien, Edward W.	22	Clerk	"
7	O'Brien, William	51	Laborer	"
11	Carey, Thomas J.	51	Gardener	480 Concord ave.
21	Leonard, Fred C.	23	Bookkeeper	same
21	Leonard, John F.	53	Foreman	"

THOMAS STREET.

No.	Name.	Age.	Occupation.	Residence 1914.
23	Egan, Patrick J.	42	Brakeman	same
25	McCormick, John	35	Carpenter	Cambridge
39	Keefe, Timothy	27	Fireman	same
39	Keefe, Thomas	54	Gardener	"
43	Collins, Thomas	70	Gate tender	Pleasant st.
47	Burnock, Patrick	30	Laborer	same
47	Douglas, Arthur L.	44	Coachman	"
53	Johnson, Frederick	33	Egg lighter	"
55	Maguire, John	38	Engineer	Somerville
57	Powers, John E.	50	Rigger	same
59	Cohen, Michael	53	Cigar maker	"
)ff	Butchard, David	56	Stone cutter	"
)ff	Butchard, David	36	" "	
)ff	Blanchard, Munroe A.	36	Inspector	
70	Shedd, Herman	21	Clerk	
68	Menard, Joseph	43	Cigar maker	
62	Sherman, Henry	48	" "	
62	Costine, Patrick	48	Laborer	
62	McNulty, Edward	28	Teamster	
62	Sliney, John	35	"	"
62	Sliney, Edward	37	Conductor	267 Waverley st.
60	Quigley, James A.	38	Milk dealer	same
60	Quigley, Edward A.	32	" "	"
60	Fuller, Royal	38	Laborer	"
56	Quigley, Edward F.	50	Baggage master	
56	Quigley, Patrick	82	Retired	
54	Friedel, Herman H.	40	Ivory worker	
52	Nickerson, Samuel	41	Chauffeur	
52	Callabro, Joseph	60	Laborer	
48	O'Connor, Jeremiah	81	Retired	
46	King, Gilbert A.	25	Clerk	
26	Arno, Joseph	28	Laborer	
26	Arno, Tony	32	"	
6	McQuaid, James	31	"	
4	Kennedy, Andrew	40	Machinist	
2	Carney, James E.	36	Laborer	

TROWBRIDGE STREET.

No.	Name.	Age.	Occupation.	Residence 1914.
	De Stefano, F.	39	Tailor	same
	Mondello, Joseph	54	Laborer	"
17	Mahan, James	49	"	"
34	Bruno, Salvator	32	Farmer	"
30	Whalen, Michael J.	57	Grocer	317 Brighton st.
30	Whalen, Andrew J.	27	Accountant	" "
24	Sagie, Joseph	27	Laborer	Boston
24	Franscali, Guy	26	"	same
24	Sacro, John	34	"	"
24	Boucher, Joseph L.	32	"	Cambridge

TROWBRIDGE STREET, - Continued.

No.	Name.	Age.	Occupation.	Residence 1914.
22	Faircloth, Wm. F.	50	Laborer	same
20	Pisaturo, Carmine	57	Fruit dealer	"
20	DeVito, A. Ralph	24	Laborer	"

UNDERWOOD STREET.

9	Pasquale, Antro	27	Laborer	same
9	Melino, Andrew	40	"	"
13	Randall, Tony	60	"	Roxbury
17	Delmastro, Dominick	42	Engineer	17 Baker st.
17	La Haie, David	53	Laborer	same
21	Bennett, Godfrey	50	"	"
21	Bennett, Edmund	21	Clerk	same
21	Crowley, John J.	49	Engineer	"
21	King, Louis	41	Mason	"
23	Baptiste, Saveno	33	Brickmaker	
27	Nichols, Patrick	57	Laborer	
27	Tibeau, Peter	40	"	
63	Driscoll, Thomas	21	Salesman	
63	Driscoll, Henry	57	Engineer	

WASHINGTON STREET.

306	White, Edward	58	Milk dealer	same
306	Cotter, Michael	25	Teamster	"
286	Richardson, William	41	Market gardener	"
232	Holt, Rollin L.	52	" "	
184	Fletcher, Elmer A.	54		
162	Stone, Walter H.	62	Retired	
80	Long, Alfred H.	42	Market gardener	
52	Chenery, Charles E.	74	Farmer	
52	Chenery, George W.	65	"	

WAVERLEY STREET.

247	Harris, Thomas F.	33	Inspector	same
247	Hatch, Edward W.	55	Express messenger	"
247	Mahoney, Robert V.	36	Electrician	"
249	Wells, Jeremiah B.	32	Letter carrier	"
251	Cormey, Alexander	22	Printer	228 Waverley st.
251	Cormey, Frederick J.	20	"	"
253	Condon, Timothy	38	Chauffeur	same
253	Keenan, Patrick J.	47	Police officer	"
257	Rhynd, Robert M.	42	Gardener	"
263	Tracy, John J.	29	Secretary	"
263	Gleason, John J.	38	Postal clerk	9 Woodland st.

WAVERLEY STREET, - Continued.

No.	Name.	Age.	Occupation.	Residence 1914
263	Perry, Leon	23	Civil engineer	same
267	Sliney, John	42	Contractor	"
269	Looney, James	32	Clerk	"
271	Looney, Timothy F.	41	Letter carrier	
275	Looney, Edward J.	43	Supt. Water Dept.	
281	Carney, John J.	46	Cabinet maker	"
299	Emery, James W.	73	Retired	Cambridge
323	Loud, John A.	40	Musician	same
331	Kimball, Thomas F.	42	Sales manager	"
343	Young, Herbert	42	Manufacturer	"
	Weston, Geo. W.	49	Actor	
308	Barrett, Fred O.	66	Agent Adams Ex. Co.	"
228	Burrows, Gordon	32	Ivory worker	34 Trowbridge st.
228	Shipley, Charles P.	56	Engineer	" "
226	McMahon, Patrick T.	43	Contractor	same
214	Daly, John	48	Laborer	"

WELLINGTON AVENUE.

No.	Name.	Age.	Occupation.	Residence 1914
33	Walton, Perry	45	Printer	same

WELLINGTON STREET.

No.	Name.	Age.	Occupation.	Residence 1914
	Kendall, Charles P.	42	Instructor	Conn.
	Rand, Earl P.	26	Grocer	Boston
	Monaghan, Edward W.	65	Mason	Dorchester

NOTE.--The word "same" refers to the street of last year's residence, the number not always being the same.

PRECINCT 2.

A STREET.

No.	Name.	Age.	Occupation.	Residence 1914.
1	Castino, Pedro	40	Driver	same
5	Lisano, Maurice	39	Florist	"
5	Perino, Joe	39	"	"
7	Natale, Laneia	26	Farm hand	Walnut st.
9	Puleio, Nunzio	44	Milkman	same

AGASSIZ AVENUE.

No.	Name.	Age.	Occupation.	Residence 1914.
7	Harris, Judson I.	56	Lineman	East Acton
7	Hennessy, John T.	34	Mail clerk	same
7	Murphy, Patrick B.	41	Shoemaker	Natick
9	Bowman, William O.	41	Meat cutter	Waltham
9	Snow, Alfred J.	21	Clerk	Boston
9	Fleming, William	26	Mechanical dentistry	"
9	Fleming, David J.	64	Retired	"
9	Grant, John F.	26	Express agent	same
35	Hubbard, William M.	34	Salesman	"
39	Aiken, William	43	Electrician	"
47	Murphy, Andrew J.	30	Janitor	
51	Tingley, Charles H.	60	Carpenter	
57	Smith, Wm. H.	26	Roofer	
74	Young, Archibald F. R.	49	Iron worker	
68	Coleman, Daniel	38	Fireman	
68	Cody, Hugh	39	Printer	
64	Adams, Erle	32	Watchman	"
56	Mason, George E.	30	Clerk	"
56	Mahoney, Henry F.	24	Time-keeper	Pleasant st.
52	Scribner, Frederick W.	41	Decorator	same
48	Adams, Franklin	48	Detective	"
26	Major, Alfred E.	33	Mason tender	Roxbury
26	Major, Arthur H.	30	Clerk	"
26	McMahon, Ambrose	30	Carpenter	15 Moraine st.
8	Redfield, Irving L.	32	Bookkeeper	20 Moraine st.
8	Westphal, August	45	Tailor	same
6	Waterbury, Wm.	35	Bookkeeper	"

AGASSIZ STREET.

No.	Name.	Age.	Occupation.	Residence 1914.
11	Mullen, Seymour H.	25	Clerk	Boston
11	Clancy, Norman N.		Bookkeeper	same
67	Carson, Robert A.	27	Automobile repairer	"
67	Bailey, Alfred	90	Retired	"

ALMA AVENUE.

No.	Name.	Age.	Occupation.	Residence 1914.
49	Stone, Fred	25	Carpenter	Dorchester
49	Stone, Chas. A.	32	Starter	same
51	Harper, Frank W.	33	Civil engineer	"
54	Bourden, Samuel	39	Carpenter	"
48	Parsons, Albert E.	70	Tailor	"
40	Gunn, Ernest D. B.		Shipping clerk	Boston
38	Minty Keywood C.	25	Builder	48 Bartlett ave.
8	Moore, Mark	30	Carpenter	same

ASH STREET.

No.	Name.	Age.	Occupation.	Residence 1914.
14	Burke, Daniel		Plumber	same

B STREET.

No.	Name.	Age.	Occupation.	Residence 1914.
5	Mazzeo, Anthony	42	Laborer	82 Beech st.
5	Gray, Jos.	44	Laborer	A street
7	Augustine, Frank	38	Farm hand	Italy
7	Ali, Joseph	28	Rubber worker	Mt. Auburn
7	Constanino, Salvator	51	Mechanic	Boston
7	Bonan, Peter	31	Laundryman	"
9	Marando, Patsy	21	Farm hand	Thomas st.
9	Smedile, Andrew	28	Laundryman	Cambridge
9	Dasma, Antro	22	Laborer	"
9	Lettiere, Dominick	25	Farm hand	Italy
9	Lettiere, Rocky	28	Shoe worker	Boston
9	Restano, Rocky	46	Farm hand	Italy

BARTLETT AVENUE.

No.	Name.	Age.	Occupation.	Residence 1914.
27	Peabody, John S.	45	Tel. inspector	same
31	Smith, Fred E.	54	Janitor	"
92	Grassie, Wm. S.	34	Florist	"
88	Taylor, John	29	Fish dealer	
48	Earle, Arthur J.	24	Carpenter	
48	Minty, Albion	42	"	
28	Wien, Paul A.	33	Electrical engineer	
	Hull, Charles B.	26	Salesman	"
	McLaughlin, Dennis	25	Conductor	111 Sycamore st.

BARTLETT ROAD.

No.	Name.	Age.	Occupation.	Residence 1914.
17	Anderson, James H.	29	Telegrapher	58 Harriet ave.
28	Davis, Harry C.	40	Designer	Somerville
16	Freeto, John F., Jr.	29	Salesman	Boston
10	Highley, Philip	67	Bookkeeper	same
10	Highly, Robert	20	Clerk	"
4	Thomas, Clifton G.	40	"	146 Beech st.

BEECH STREET.

No.	Name.	Age.	Occupation.	Residence 1914.
75	McAllister, John J.	46	Supt.	215 White st.
77	Jack, Wm. A.	50	Cabinet maker	same
79	Olsson, Jacob	37	Teamster	East Boston
83	Brant, Isaac	45	Janitor	same
83	Brant, Arthur	37	Painter	"
83	MacKenzie, John G.	44	Carpenter	"
83	Barrett, Joseph F.	32	Fruit dealer	Manchester, N.H.
85	Schliephake, Robert H.	32	Piano maker	same
85	Holmes, Wm. H.	29	Clerk	"
85	Pliskin, Solomon	50	Tailor	Boston
85	Pliskin, David	21	Salesman	"
91	Taylor, Walter D.	31	Carpenter	24 Francis st.
91	Blake, Harry E.	50	Manager	Newton
91	Alt, James	40	Chauffeur	Allston
91	Sheehan, Daniel F.	44	Carpenter	Newtonville
93	Pierpont, Frank	33	Milkman	220 White st.
93	Cupid, Alex.	30	Nurse	Boston
93	Hanson, Martin P.	28	Salesman	Medford
95	Stewart, John	52	Carpenter	Watertown
95	Heuser, Emil	35	Frame-maker	School st.
99	Mosher, John L.	39	Teamster	9 Davis road
99	Marchmond, Chas. M.	40	Painter	Trapelo road
99	Fogerty, James L.	22	Insurance	same
99	Ford, Walter F.	32	Blacksmith	Watertown
99	Duffley, James F.	23	Bakery	West Orange, N.J.
101	Stuart, Everett J.	22	Optician	same
101	Stuart, Chas. W.	32	Salesman	"
101	Lippe, Raoul J.	45	Architect	Cambridge
101	Westcott, James H.	39	Teamster	So. Boston
103	Kerrigan, John	45	Watchman	same
103	McBride, James	24	Pressman	"
103	McBride, John	23	Stenographer	"
105	Conlon, Joseph L.	32	Gardener	Roxbury
105	Kaplan, George	32	Manager	Cambridge
107	Middleton, Benjamin	47	Engineer	12 Sycamore st.
107	Coén, Michael	48	Motorman	same
107	Shea, John F.	30	Electrician	U. S. Navy
117	Dickerson, John	28	Watchmaker	Cambridge
121	Brown, Chester P.	30	Physician	"
123	Chism, John	38	Salesman	Somerville
147	Marks, Thomas W.	57	Stockfitter	same
149	Small, Chas. C.	33	Letter carrier	"
151	Nichols, Jonathan E.	33	Manufacturer	"
153	Rodd, Harry C.	22	Electrotype finisher	"
155	Fisher, John R.	67	Auditor	Boston
155	Gough, Edward J.	24	Bookkeeper	Boston
159	Mann, Wallace R.	24	Marketman	164 Beech st.
161	Kelley, James T.	30	Machinist	same
163	Becker, William C.	45	Brass finisher	"
165	Boulcott, John T.	52	" "	"

BEECH STREET, - Continued.

No.	Name.	Age.	Occupation.	Residence 1914
171	Crook, Robert	36	Bookkeeper	same
171	Talbot, Walter J.	33	Clerk	"
171	Engstrom, Herman A.	35	Mason	"
175	Johnson, Werner E.	30	Carpenter	"
175	MacAuliffe, Florence	40	Inspector (stoves)	Watertown
200	Angelo, Frank	40	Grocer	same
172	Gervais, Stanislas	31	Organ builder	"
172	White, Edward K.	27	Salesman	"
164	Balough, Bertram	45	Cabinet maker	Wilson ave.
164	Swanson, Nils P.	43	Carpenter	same
158	Harrington, Chas. S.	54	Bookkeeper	Boston
156	Gowey, Fred L.	52	Foreman	29 Wilson ave.
154	Penn, Geo. J.	34	Insurance	same
154	French, Joseph B.	60	Pressman	"
152	Gardner, Andrew J.	68	Electrician	"
150	Towne, Joseph L.	53	Druggist	82 Lexington st.
150	Strout, Vernon L.	24	"	" " "
148	Callahan, Henry F.	42	Grocer	same
146	Harrington, Albert D.	22	Instructor	"
146	Moorehead, Geo. A.	25	Printer	Cambridge
146	Harrington, Albert H.	60	Painter	same
140	Anderson, Lars A.	39	Carpenter	"
140	Stockwell, Geo. P.	50	Salesman	"
140	Dresser, Geo.	26	Organ	Trapelo road
138	Landall, Charles R.	26	Teacher	same
138	Landall, Abel E.	20	Jobber	"
138	Johnson, Christenson	55	Engineer	"
138	Beekman, James G.	32	Pattern maker	"
138	Landall, Simon P.	30	Cutter (clothing)	48 Falmouth st.
124	Argy, John	58	Police officer	same
122	Lawton, Fred H.	35	Asst. Supt.	"
92	Parker, John N.	24	Cabinet maker	Cambridge
88	Kearns, Michael	62	Blacksmith	same
88	Kearns, Joseph	28	"	"
82	Pompino, Chas.	29	Druggist	Church st.

BELMONT STREET.

No.	Name.	Age.	Occupation.	Residence 1914
577	Williston, Samuel	56	Professor	same
583	Richert, Henry C.	32	Artist	"
603	Horne, Geoffrey	38	Farmer	"
	Bourden, John	49	Carpenter	
729	Swanson, Emil	40	Grocer	
785	Lamkin, W. R.	47	Salesman	
789	Gould, Wm. H.	58	Janitor	
811	Mackay, Edgar F.	23	Student	
811	Mackay, Hector	64	Carpenter	
813	Porter, Louis F.	40	Druggist	
	Beckman, William C.	31	Plumber	

BELMONT STREET, - Continued.

No.	Name.	Age.	Occupation.	Residence 1914.
	Moulton, Arthur C.	31	Salesman	same

BENJAMIN ROAD.

	Schmuch, Bernard	50	Tailor	same
	Descoteaux, George N.	24	Accountant	Boston
	Luszcz, Martin	49	Pressman	same
	Whipple, Clarence M.	28	Claim adjuster	"
	Donle, Earl R.	25	Civil engineer	"
	Harris, Harry	36	Secretary	Mattapan

BURNHAM STREET.

19	Dennett, L. Guy	43	Lawyer	same
33	Lansil, Earl F.	41	Electrician	"
37	Scranton, Carl	42	Agent	
37	Andrews, Newell D.	31	Clerk	126 Sycamore st.
43	Andrews, Arthur W.	28	Clerk	same
43	Andrews, Edward F.	60	Engraver	"
57	Robinson, Oliver G.	37	Upholstering	"
54	Cox, William T.	43	Postmaster	
54	Purington, George C.	34	Manager	"
52	Landall, E. Lawrence	32	Carpenter	Davis road
52	Andrews, Everett E.	30	Salesman	same
52	Parker, Percy C.	37	Salesman	33 Burnham st.
46	Little, Waldo F.	54	Clerk	same
42	Macomber, Eugene T.	54	Machinist	"
34	Oakes, John H.	35	Clerk	"
28	Edwards, John	57	Clerk	
22	Claus, Robert C.	55	Salesman	"
12	Taylor, Henry W.	28	Buyer	1 Chestnut st.
12	Newcomb, John W.	78	Retired	same

CAMBRIDGE STREET.

13	Baer, Anton	58	Furrier	same
13	Baer, Otto	21	"	"
20	Dole, Albion B.	56	Machinist	Trapelo road
20	Lewis, Augustus H.	55	Watchman	same
18	Morrill, Rexford D.	24	Electrician	"
16	Walsh, Matthew J.	40	Baggage master	"
10	Young, George W.	76	Retired	
4	Melanson, Joseph E.	48	Confectioner	

CHANDLER STREET.

15	Whitehill, Walter M.	34	Manager	same

CHANDLER STREET, - Continued.

No.	Name.	Age.	Occupation.	Residence 1914
25	Fitzgerald, John	37	Pressman	Cambridge
27	Fisher, Hugh	54	Stone cutter	same
33	Lever, Geo. W.	49	Metal polisher	" "
45	Fisher, James	60	Market gardener	" "
45	Fisher, James H.	21	" " " "	
59	Moore, W. H.	54	Carpenter	
50	Lietz, Carl	29	Florist	
50	Carlo, Joseph	34	Laborer	
46	Sullivan, Simon	42	Chauffeur	" "
20	Burleigh, Charles	60	Physician	Cambridge
20	Burleigh, Willard G.	20	Mechanical engineer	" " "
18	Keegan, James F.	41	Coachman	same
16	Cogan, William H.	30	Clerk	" "
16	Davis, Allan M.	51	Stationer	" "

CHESTNUT STREET.

No.	Name.	Age.	Occupation.	Residence 1914
5	Templay, Edmund T.	36	Dental supplies	Milton
	Wright, George C.	52	Painter	210 Waverley st.

CHURCH STREET.

No.	Name.	Age.	Occupation.	Residence 1914
16	Daly, M. J.	49	Shipper	same
16	Dutcher, C. F.	42	Salesman	" "
16	Keegan, W. H.	48	Livery	Thayer st.
16	MacLeod, Alexander	41	Carpenter	same
ff	Hernon, Patrick T.	65	Janitor	" "
24	Brown, E. Horace	38	Engineer	" "
36	Harding, Frederick	21	Printer	
36	Coleman, J. E.	40	Station agent	
40	Snow, Augustus W.	40	Salesman	

CHURCH STREET PLACE.

No.	Name.	Age.	Occupation.	Residence 1914
	Priest, Charles M.	30	Designer	same
	Harrison, Benjamin S.	48	Steamfitter	" "
	Harrison, John T.	43	Bookkeeper	" "
	Young, Frank E.	46	Driver	" "
	Whitney, William R.	30	" "	Watertown

COMMON STREET.

No.	Name.	Age.	Occupation.	Residence 1914
325	Chenery, Franklin W.	39	Farmer	same
325	Chenery, David	76	" "	" "
ff	Slade, Walter H.	33	Market gardener	" "

COMMON STREET - Continued.

No.	Name.	Age.	Occupation.	Residence 1914.
375	Creeley, Thomas L.	65	Market gardener	same
455	Carson, James S.	55	Coachman	"
455	Carson, James	21	Clerk	"
489	Philbuck, Otis	26	School teacher	Revere
497	Gay, Harry D.	33	Teamster	same

CONCORD AVENUE.

	Brown, Edward A.	74	Farmer	same
	Fillebrown, Warren A.	34	"	"

CREELEY ROAD.

25	Magnuson, Bernard	27	Engraver	same
25	Honeth, Gustaf G.	33	Carpenter	"
25	Maloon, Fred	22	Electrician	"
52	Johnson, August	40	Piano finisher	
50	Nestor, Michael	35	Laborer	"
48	Hackett, Francis	22	Machinist	Allston
	Johnson,	33	Clerk	same
	Gunning, Thomas	34	Teamster	"

CUTTER STREET.

11	Beverly, Geo. W.	53	Interior decorator	same
11	Flanders, Charles E.	31	Telephone manager	"
11	Harrod, W. T.	53	Railroad (Special agt.)	"
17	Allen, Charles A. Rev.	77	Clergyman	"
17	Fagan, James O.	56	Railroad man	610 Trapelo rd.
25	McNeil John H.	51	Motorman	same
25	Collins, Nelson A.	30	Electrical engineer	Newton
27	Haigh, Wm.	28	Grocer	159 Beech st.
27	Blodgett, Geo. E.	39	Garage owner	20 Chandler st.
27	Mershon, Stephen L.	28	Salesman	1 Chestnut st.
26	Scott, James P.	48	Printer	same
24	Knapp, Frank S.	32	Bookkeeper	"
20	Alcock, Samuel	35	Builder	"
16	Rounsefelt, Guy P.	28	Salesman	
10	Goodwin, Morris H.	35	Supt.	"
10	Goodwin, Samuel H.	70	Retired	Lexington

DAVID ROAD.

	Nesie, Joe	49	Laborer	same
	Kakefiro, Bastin	45	"	"
	Restuicco, Dominic	46	"	"

DAVID ROAD - Continued.

No.	Name.	Age.	Occupation.	Residence 1914.
	Anastas, Tony	26	Laborer	same
	Ollis, Harry	40	Mechanic	" "
	Johnson, Kimball	27	Clerk	" "
	Cherry, Charles W.	26	Auto salesman	
	Sparrow, W. A.	35	Cabinet maker	
	Cherry, Thomas H.	34	Shipping clerk	
64	Phelps, Harry E.	40	Carpenter	
64	Brassil, John E.	31	Letter carrier	
	Jacobson, Fridolf M.	29	Investigator	
	Jacobson, Joseph H.	25	Clerk	
	Jacobson, Henning Rev.	58	Clergyman	

DAVIS ROAD.

No.	Name.	Age.	Occupation.	Residence 1914.
7	Deehan, Frank E.	26	Manager	Boston
7	Smith, Nelson J.	66	Machinist	13 Davis st.
9	Murray, Wm. H.	45	Letter carrier	40 Waverley st.
11	Kelly, Fred	35	Teamster	21 Francis st.
11	Kierstead, Geo. A.	56	Carpenter	342 Trapelo road
19	Craig, Joseph	36	Shipping clerk	Brookline
21	Fulton. John E.	36	Plumber	same
24	Duncan, Oscar W.	34	Teacher	
22	Cherry, Leslie R.	32	Painter	329 Trapelo road
22	Buckley, Prescott	24	"	same
22	Buckley, Daniel	26	"	" "
22	Buckley, John	28	Milk business	" "
16	Murtaugh, William J.	31	Purchasing agt.	Cambridge
14	Forand, Delphis C.	40	Carpenter	Creeley road
12	Parker, Urban J.	20	Insurance	same
12	Davison, F. A.	23	Clerk	Boston
12	Parker, Urban	47	Insurance	same
10	Potter, Frank S.	55	Roofer	" "

DAVIS STREET.

No.	Name.	Age.	Occupation.	Residence 1914.
15	Furlong, William J.	41	Treasurer	same

DREW ROAD.

No.	Name.	Age.	Occupation.	Residence 1914.
	Hagerty, Eugene	21	Stenographer	280 Waverley st.

FRANCIS STREET.

No.	Name.	Age.	Occupation.	Residence 1914.
17	Chapman, Loring T.	27	Electrician	339 Trapelo road
19	Morris, Harold W.	35	Asst. manager	same

FRANCIS STREET, - Continued.

No.	Name.	Age.	Occupation.	Residence 1914.
21	Hazelton, Chas.	28	Motorman	same
23	McMurdie, Orgin A.	36	Clerk	Dorchester
25	Carlton, Chas. E.	32	Merchant	327 Trapelo road
27	Winship, Harry H.	35	Machinist	Watertown
29	Fairbanks, James	24	Salesman	same
31	Curry, Joseph A.	29	Druggist	295 Lexington st
12	Littlejohn, Albert V.	21	Clerk	Boston
12	Littlejohn, George J.	23	Stenographer	" "
12	Littlejohn, James	66	Machinist	" "
10	McLaughlin, Joseph F.	40	Steamfitter	28 Maple st.

FREDERICK STREET.

No.	Name.	Age.	Occupation.	Residence 1914.
18	Baker, Alden F.	50	Foreman	same
12	Goneau, Alphonse A. J.	32	Architect	99 Beech st.
10	Dillon, Albert W.	42	Carpenter	same
10	Stevens, Chas. B.	38	Clerk	No. Abington

GRANT AVENUE.

No.	Name.	Age.	Occupation.	Residence 1914.
9	Delagatto, James	30	Farm hand	same
9	Venuti, John	30	" "	"
13	Desmond. Patrick	35	Laborer	Maine
13	Desmond, Jeremiah	37	"	same
15	Bella, John	29	"	"
15	Galatti, Joseph	56	Farm hand	"
17	Laspada, Antonio	48	"	
17	Andrelo, John	20	Laborer	
17	Fonte, Salvatore	24	"	
17	Oteri, Antonio	72	Retired	
17	Oteri, Gregorio	39	Teamster	
19	Scarfo, Salvatore	32	Laborer	
57	Dally, John	43	Jobber	··
59	Smedili, Peter	28	Laborer	
59	Napoli, Antonio	35	"	
70	Oikemus, John	32	"	
52	Carlo, Peter	32		
52	Annuziata, Luigi	28	"	
48	Parisi, Anthony	27	Iron moulder	
48	Macolini, Frank	31	Laborer	"
42	Dadeski, Philip	26	"	Boston
42	Maffei, Michael	34	"	same
38	Alberto, Carnio	55		"
36	Lomadico, Michael	28	"	"
34	Ramobln, Gene	46		
32	Fermia, Nicholas	49		
24	Telford, William	54		

HARRIET AVENUE.

No.	Name.	Age.	Occupation.	Residence 1914.
11	Gustafson, Gunner S.	27	Wood carver	same
11	Gustafson, Samuel	52	Carpenter	"
11	Gustafson, Emanuel	25	Draughtsman	"
11	Gustafson, Fred	23	Photographer	
11	Reid, Peter M.	45	Carpenter	
17	Knibb, Albert E.	45	Traffic manager	"
27	Barnes, George H.	59	Builder	408 Trapelo road
27	Barnes, Wales C.	23	"	" " "
29	Rock, Harry		Teller	same
39	Marshall, Aubrey M.	35	Laundryman	Cambridge
47	Gordon, Ira H.	46	Carpenter	same
51	Colburn, Chas. L.	48	Carpenter	"
53	Murdock, Joseph	25	Geologist	Allston
60	Dodge, George H.	30	Supt.	same
58	Clark, Walter B.	22	Student and Teacher	Cambridge
58	Clark, Lyman, O.	48	Custom Service	Cambridge
20	Blaisdell, Warren H.	30	Buyer	same
16	Mills, Chas.	47	Electrical contractor	"

HAWTHORN STREET.

No.	Name.	Age.	Occupation.	Residence 1914.
19	Barney, Chas.	52	Janitor	same
29	Rotchford, James F.	22	Carpenter's helper	"
29	Doyle, Edmund	44	Plumber	"
39	Sanicariello, Tobia	53	Fruit dealer	
43	McDermott, Michael E.	26	Fireman	
43	McDermott, Timothy J.	57	Gardener	
47	Knight, John W.	56	Postal clerk	
36	Griffith, Norman H.	34	Broker	
30	Dutra, Joseph J.	44	Barber	
16	Kewer, Wm. J.	50	Baker and news dealer	"
16	Kewer, Howard	21	Student	
6	Kellogg, Alfred S.	48	Merchant	

HENRY STREET.

Name.	Age.	Occupation.	Residence 1914.
Murphy, Patrick J.	40	Blacksmith	same
McDermott, Joseph H.	31	Towerman	"

HOLT STREET.

No.	Name.	Age.	Occupation.	Residence 1914.
17	Bowler, Herbert W.	30	Lumber dealer	27 Cutter st.
35	Upham, Thomas	80	Manufacturer	same
35	Thomas, Wm. H.	42	Plasterer	"
37	Thomas, Chester R.	20	"	"
18	Peckham, Albert B.	43	Trav. salesman	

HOLT STREET, - Continued.

No.	Name.	Age.	Occupation.	Residence 1914.
16	Simm, Fred E.	33	Dentist	same
16	Kendall, Walter S.	49	Gardener	"
10	Reeves, F. H.	61	Clerk	"
10	Cummings, John J.	32	Collector (Met. Life Ins.)	"

HULL STREET.

No.	Name.	Age.	Occupation.	Residence 1914.
9	Boissonade, Chas. J.	45	Watchmaker	same
9	Woods, Herbert S.	37	Chauffeur	"
9	Coen, Dennis M.	29	Motorman	Waltham
45	Jolin, Simon G.	74	Builder	same
63	Garber, Robert A.		Clerk	"
63	Curley, Owen S.	28	Conductor	Boston
63	Hankard, Edward T.	58	Chef	9 Hull st.
87	Bucci, Donato	33	Upholsterer	42 Grant ave.
87	Scarfo, Vincenzo	46	Farm hand	" " "
66	Restuccia, John	40	Laborer	same
64	Santagiato, Nino	32	Farm hand	Waltham
64	Tricone, Gregorio	32	" "	same
8	Olsson, Chas.	45	Laborer	Cambridge
6	Reynolds, Michael J.	40	"	same

IRVING STREET.

No.	Name.	Age.	Occupation.	Residence 1914.
	Hubbard, Perley O.	31	Bookkeeper	416 Trapelo road
	Lufkin, Edwin F.	30	Salesman	" " "

JEANETTE AVENUE.

No.	Name.	Age.	Occupation.	Residence 1914.
36	Malenfant, Joseph F.	49	Artist	}
34	Mann, David W.	27	Mechanic	}

LEXINGTON STREET.

No.	Name.	Age.	Occupation.	Residence 1914.
11	Mercer, Nathan	26	Carpenter	Cambridge
11	Eisnor, Fred A.	34	Store-keeper	same
11	King, Frank L.	31	Photographer	"
11	Andrews, Eben F.	32	Clerk	"
41	Arnold, Chas. A.	30	Salesman	
41	Fisher, John	53	Clerk	
43	Edgar, John	65	Florist	
45	Hinton, John R.	42	Clerk	
45	Gibson, Henry T.	26	"	
45	Gibson, Thomas H.	51	Engineer	"
75	Brown, James J.	35	Glazier	439 Trapelo road

LEXINGTON STREET, - Continued.

No.	.	Name.	Age.	Occupation.	Residence 1914
75		McBride, John	22	Chef	439 Trapelo road
75		Bryan, Fred	27	Reporter	Waltham
75		Johnson, Frank	28	Machinist	"
75		O'Donnell, Michael	26	Florist	Boston
75		McCanagher, Thomas	26	Steamfitter	439 Trapelo road
75		Lyons, John S.	28	Drug clerk	Montreal
75		Lyons, Patrick	30	Clerk	Fitchburg
77		Nutter, Chas. A.	32	P. O. clerk	same
79		Patriquin, Burton	47	Shipper	"
81		Moore, Geo. E.	54	Contractor	"
81		Ellis Leopold	46	Iron dealer	
83		Woods, William M.	34	Clerk	
83		Nickerson, Wm. A.	29	Teacher	
91		Scott, Chas. S.	60	Real estate	"
115		Christie, William H.	36	Provisions	Somerville
119		Wilson, John	46	Manufacturer	same
141		Hall, Robert H.	20	Student	"
141		Hall, Malcolm B.	27	Mechanical engineer	Lowell
141		Hall, Wesley G.	54	Hatter	same
147		Ellis, J. Lucius	70	Broker	"
181		Corey, Fred A.	47	Salesman	"
201		Ryan, C. Tracy	22	Clerk	
201		Ryan, Walter D.	51	Foreman	
211		Holmes, Fred L.	58	Manufacturer	
219		Henry, Danford T.	72	Retired	
220		Haskins, Fred	41	Broker	
214		Holscher, Harry	29	Sign painter	
214		Holscher, Henry A.	53	" "	
214		Holscher, Edwin	25	Artist	
212		Manson, Warren	52	Carpenter	"
212		Collinson, Claude M. B.	32	Manager	Watertown
206		Russell, Herbert H.	65	Supt. post office	same
198		Pierce, Chas. W.	50	Fireman	"
190		Tucker, Warren W.	47	Broker	"
174		Sprague, Wm.	75	Retired	27 Cutter st.
174		Crocker, Robert	33	Salesman	" " "
172		Marsh, Wm. P.	47	Piano manufacturer	same
120		Burke, Michael J.	30	Gardener	"
90		Chandler, F. Alexander	34	Merchant	"
84		Hayden, Frank A.	20	Salesman	
84		Carr, Oliver F.	47	Dentist	
76		McKenzie, Forbes	52	Contractor	
76		McKenzie, Geo. L.	22	"	
60		Green, Wm.	32	Student	
50		Crowell, Clarence	50	Mariner	
50		Andrews, Frank	39	Clerk	
50		Goodwin, Gilbert A.	56	Paper hanger	
46		DeMond, Geo. A.	66	Printer	"
46		Atwell, Andrew Y.	27	Manager	Dorchester
46		DeMond, Frank S.	27	Watchmaker	same

LEXINGTON STREET, - Continued.

No.	Name.	Age.	Occupation.	Residence 1914.
42	Russell, Clarence A.	36	Clerk	same
40	Sherburne, John R.	52	Teamster	"
38	Maynard, Elmer W.	20	Elevator man	"

MAPLE STREET.

9	Shaughnessy, Daniel R.	28	Milk dealer	same
9	Shaughnessy, Eugene	33	Clerk	"
9	Shaughnessy, Thomas	28	Milk dealer	"
11	Beecher, Wm. J.	27	Conductor	Cambridge
13	Atkinson, Wm. T.	42	Engineer	same
17	Kearns, Edward J.	38	Postal clerk	"
25	Loumos, Anast	60	Grocer clerk	"
43	Meehan, Geo.	27	Expressman	
43	Underhill, Henry	29	Real estate	Lowell
47	Beals, Wm.	26	Mechanical iron worker	27 Park road
47	Whittemore, Earl C.	25	Clerk	327 Trapelo road
51	Abbott, Frank A.	36	Teamster	Medford
51	Leland, Clarence E.	27	Tel. engineer	Cambridge
55	Overlan, John J.	33	Clerk	E. Boston
55	Bunker, John P.	26	Bank clerk	Cambridge
40	Jordan, Joseph	32	Laborer	same
40	Addessa, Tony	46	"	"
36	Channal, William	40	Engineer	215 White st.
36	Hennessey, John	60	Farmer	same
34	Gitelson, Hyman	30	Painter	"
34	Burns, Edward A.	27	Mechanic	"
32	Esters Clarence E.	35	Bookbinder	
32	Fogarty, George F.	26	Bricklayer	"
28	Shaughnessy, Patrick J.	39	Conductor	
24	Silber, Isaac		Merchant	Boston
24	Sorkin, Jacob	34	Carpenter	same
24	Wallace, William T.	42	Laborer	"
24	Wallace, William O.	20	Driver	"
	McRoberts, William M.	42	Gardener	

MAPLE TERRACE

7	Walsh, Michael	54	Fireman	same
7	Walsh, Wm.	23	Laborer	"
9	Nichols, Wm. H.	28	Shipper	"
9	Gosewisch, Frederick A.L.	38	Salesman	Boston
13	Wilson, J. W.	38	Manufacturer	10 Francis st.
13	Johnson, Harris S.	36	Laundryman	same
17	Murphy, Dennis	45	Laborer	"
17	Daley, P. J.	52	Retired	"
17	Daley, John	25	Conductor	

MIDLAND STREET

No.	Name.	Age.	Occupation.	Residence 1914.
14	Donahue, Thomas	32	Conductor	same
14	Donahue, Patrick	66	Laborer	"
14	Donahue, William	30	Conductor	"
14	Donahue, Robert	24	Plumber	
12	Grant, Edward F.	51	Chef	
12	Grant, William H.	22	Express driver	

MILL STREET.

165	Hock, Theodore A.	36	Physician	same
251	Magoon, Henry E.	38	Supervisor	"
319	Burdakin, Gilbert	34	Electrician	"
319	Burdakin, Arthur L.	65	Farmer	
248	Stanley, John D.	42	Foreman	
248	Curley, Mitchell	35	Farm hand	
248	Strange, Edgar	27	" "	
248	Johnson, Hugh	38	" "	
248	Rowe, Claude	30	" "	
248	Stratton, George	42	" "	
248	Quinn, Mitchell	25	" "	
178	Kendall, J. Henry	44	Merchant	
178	Kendall, Geo.	76	Retired	
178	Kendall, Geo. A.	46	"	
154	Seaver, Robert	42	Printer	
146	Kendall, G. Fred	57	Farmer	
66	Elder, Robert T.	75	Park supt.	

MORAINE STREET.

7	Bent, Guy	23	Instructor	Trapelo road
7	Wellsman, J. C.	65	Painter	same
9	Pasley, Wm. A.	29	Machinist	"
11	Andrews, Harry A.	28	Clerk	"
15	Ayer, Lucius A. J.	65	Produce dealer	
19	Trowbridge, Merle E.	26	Clerk	
19	Trowbridge, Wm. C.	53	Manager	"
31	Morgan, Edward D.	57	Mechanic	Waltham
31	Jackson, Frank H.	43	Salesman	same
33	Carter, Edward A.	45	Telegrapher	"
35	Holton, Cheney J.	26	Manager	"
37	Marie, Frank W.	37	Printer	
51	Beals, Geo. A.	55	Milk dealer	
51	Beals, Wm. A.	22	" "	"
53	Scott, Edward H.	35	Cashier	51 Moraine st.
38	Bartsch, Herman H.	42	Florist	same
20	Haskell, George H.	40	Adjuster	
20	Barrows, James A.	74	Retired	Quincy

MORAINE STREET, - Continued.

No.	Name.	Age.	Occupation.	Residence 1914.
20	Hough, Arthur E.	35	Paymaster	same
20	Wilcomb, Charles L.	42	Electrician	Cambridge
20	Barrows, Alvin S.	39	Paper hanger	Quincy
20	Mackenzie, James	37	Manager	Framingham
20	Marsh, Henry L.	38	Electrician	Cambridge
16	Desmond, William	38	Teamster	same
16	Le Blanc, William	39	Baker	"
10	McLean, Arthur	21	Fireman	Maine
10	Carroll, Leo		Teamster	Cape Bretton
10	Blanchard, Michael P.	47	Carpenter	same
6	Hughes, Philip K.	47	Blacksmith	"
6	Hughes, Chester C.	20	Clerk	"
6	Cook, Charles Sumner	20	"	Gardner

PEARL STREET.

	Name	Age	Occupation	Residence
	Gorham, William M.	22	U. S. Navy	Vera Cruz
	Gorham, Alfred M.	24	Clerk	Cambridge
5	Gorham, Nathaniel T.	48	Bookkeeper	"
	Corbett, Chas. W.	35	Purchasing agt.	Boston

PLEASANT STREET.

Name	Age	Occupation	Residence
Ahearn, John	32	Coachman	same
Annis, Frank	42	Nurse	"
Ardrie, C. Cornish	34	Fireman	Gardner
Armitage, John S.	58	Foreman	same
Balch, Geo. L.	34	Nurse	"
Bickmore, Geo.	21	"	"
Blum, Wm. J.	20	"	
Bollinger, J. Guy	20		
Bollinger, T. Frank	22	"	
Brabazon, Ed. R.	22		
Brooke, Percy A.	22		
Brown, Stephen S.	23	"	
Carmichael, Charles	30	Porter	
Carr, Paul J.	25	Steam engineer	
Chrisholm, Wm. D.	20	Nurse	
Chrisholm, Roderick A. J.	30	"	
Coole, Gerald W.	26		
Crispo, Fred.	43		
Cupid, Alex. G.	29	"	"
Daghlian, Harontune	25		
Doherty, John	23	Porter	Ireland
Eaton, Chas. A.	38	Nurse	same
Enos, George	24	Plumber	Somerville
Fadden, James	23	Fireman	Boston

PLEASANT STREET, - Continued.

No.	Name.	Age.	Occupation.	Residence 1914.
	Fagerstrowm, John	26	Nurse	same
	Farmer, Fred	26	"	"
	Frian, Thomas P.	24	Fireman	Roxbury
	Frink, Arthur H.	21	Nurse	same
	Frost, Henry E.	68	"	"
	Gordon, Elbridge W.	30	"	"
	Graham, Geo. D.	23		
	Grinnell, Elmer N.	26	"	
	Hale, Wm. Chas.	28	Fireman	
	Hogan, Francis S.	23	Nurse	
	Hoger, Fritz	43	"	
	Howell, Sidney K.	28	Apothecary	
	Huntown, Lawrence	24	Nurse	"
	Hurley, Peter	22	Porter	So. Boston
	Kennedy, Ross M.	22	Nurse	same
	Kimball, Sam A.	28	"	"
	Larson, Carl	29	Asst. chef	Cambridge
	Lawrence, Archie W.	27	Nurse	same
	Leighton, Rual J.	24	"	"
	Lewald, Oswald	24	Chauffeur	"
	Logan, Geo.	22	Nurse	
	Lawrington, Richard W.	27	"	
	Lynch, Edward F.	21	"	
	Mahiedas, John	26	Porter	
	May, John J.	23	Nurse	
	McCullock, David	25	Fireman	
	McDevitt, James	23	Asst. baker	
	McKisson, Arthur	24	Nurse	"
	McLean, Malcolm Allen	24	Fireman	
	Mercer, Alfred	38	Head porter	Los Angeles, Cal.
	Mickmeny, Thomas	24	Nurse	same
	Moran, Peter	29	Laundry work	E. Saugus
	Morse, Harold	24	Nurse	same
	Munroe, Alexander	51	Floor polisher	"
	Neal, Joseph E.	27	Nurse	
	O'Neil, William	25	Porter	Arlington
	Packard, Frederic H.	39	Physician	same
	Pooler, Howard E.	20	Nurse	"
	Quinn, Murray	23	Kitchen boy	Cambridge
	Quinn, Theodore	24	Nurse	same
	Ross, Arthur	34	"	"
	Rounsefill, Clifford Geo.	34	Physician	"
	Sammet, Joseph	22	Cook	"
	Samuelson, Oscar	23	Chauffeur	New York
	Simpson, Albert	20	Nurse	same
	Speiss, Dennis	27	Coal passer	Boston
	Telker, Leon L.	36	Nurse	same
	Tompkins, Edward	26	"	"
	Tuttle, George T.	65	Physician	"
	Waldo, Clinton F.	24	Nurse	

PLEASANT STREET, - Continued.

No.	Name.	Age.	Occupation.	Residence 1914.
	Ward, Wm. H.	23	Nurse	same
	Ward, Arthur H.	28	"	"
	Warner, Chas. B.	33	"	"
	Wateroff, George J.	34	Foreman	"
	Wells, Frederic Lyman	31	Psychologist	
	Wheeler Dan H.	20	Nurse	
	Whitney, Ray Lester	37	Physician	"
	Willis, John	25	Porter	Panama
	Wood, Geo. E.	20	Nurse	same
1034	Fleck, Matthew W.	41	P. O. clerk	"
1032	Whiting, John G.	21	Inspector	"
1032	Whiting, Thomas H.	60	Insurance	
1032	Whiting, Herbert E.	22	Clerk	
1028	Sanderson, Wm. M.	54		
1028	Sanderson, Wm. P.	89	Retired	"
1026	Kennedy, William J.	32	Merchant	Trapelo road

RIDGE ROAD.

17	Symonds, Harold V.	26	Bookkeeper	same
17	Tuttle, G. Raymond	36	Manufacturer	"
34	Brown, Frank E.	31	Clerk	Quincy
32	Connor, William N.	35	Civil engineer	Concord, Mass.
30	Landall, Phillip A.	28	Draughtsman	138 Beech st.
26	Garner, William	38	Clerk	same
22	Thompson, Edward J.	28	Entomologist	Mexico
22	Thompson, Ernest H.	26	Engineer	same
16	Sterritt, William W.	40	Collector	"

SLADE STREET.

9	Woolfrey, Gilbert	26	Carpenter	same
9	Woolfrey, George	27	"	"

SYCAMORE STREET

13	Slater, John T. H.	28	Florist	same
17	Kilpatrick, Charles W.	49	Builder	"
55	Weiler, Ernest G.	27	Clerk	"
55	Fillmore, Millard	24	"	Hudson
59	Robinson, William F.	64	Chauffeur	same
59	Perry, Joseph E.	30	Lawyer	"
61	Murphy, Edward	70	Blacksmith	"
103	Thorndike, Leonidas M.	27	Accountant	Lynn
105	Kinread, Wm. R.	62	Builder	same
107	Larrabee, Robert B.	57	Manufacturer	"

SYCAMORE STREET, - Continued.

No.	Name.	Age.	Occupation.	Residence 1914.
107	Larrabee, Everett C.	23	Manufacturer	same
107	Larrabee, Howard B.	21	Salesman	"
111	Robertson, Duncan A.	52	Florist	"
141	Beeler, Enoch F.	68	Carpenter	
143	Loomer, Frank L.	43	"	
144	Farrington, Daniel	47	Farmer	
138	Luscia,	35	Chauffeur	
136	Clarke, William J.	38	Carpenter	"
128	Flynn, John F.	60	Fireman	25 Chandler st.
128	Flynn, Andrew. F.	32	Salesman	" " "
126	McGinty, John V.	34	Printer	Cambridge
120	Sutcliffe, Everett	35	Asst. supt.	same
108	Mulvihill, Wm.	44	Foreman	"
106	Carey, Geo. H.	66	Appraiser	"
104	Carey, Ralph H.	34	Clerk	
98	Spidle, J. Lawrence	47	"	"
98	Spinney, Edmund C.	32	Nurse	McLean Hosp.
96	Cahill, Thomas P.	35	Janitor	same
96	Clark, J. Frank	39	Manager	173 White st.
94	Webster, John	27	Carpenter	same
94	Sherman, Lee	22	Salesman	"
92	Tukey, Frederick J.	38	Watchmaker	"
62	Stearns, Harry C.	30	Student	California
62	Drayton, Frank O.	28	Musician	same
60	Langley, W. F.	29	Machinist	"
36	Clark, L. B.	52	Physician	"
12	Stacey, Clifford L.	34	Foreman	Cambridge
4	Oteri, Harry R.	40	Fruit dealer	same
4	Tricone, Sebastian	34	Last carrier	1 A street

THAYER ROAD.

No.	Name.	Age.	Occupation.	Residence 1914.
40	Millward, Albert J.	34	Mail clerk	same
36	Dodge, Frank W.	34	Bookkeeper	"
22	Bryant, Melvin H.	20	Musician	"
16	Beeler, William E.	49	Cabinet maker	
16	Beeler, Fred	27	Piano factory	
16	Wallace, William	28	P. O. clerk	
14	Scottron, Samuel J.	38	" "	

THAYER STREET.

No.	Name.	Age.	Occupation.	Residence 1914.
8	Cushing, Edward O.	40	Musician	same
6	Palfrey, Charles E.	30	Bookkeeper	"
2	Winslow, Everett M.	45	Engineer	"
2	Barnes, Israel M.	30	Attendant	

TRAPELO ROAD.

No.	Name.	Age.	Occupation.	Residence 1914.
323	Nystrom, John F.	47	Baker	same
323	Nystrom, Karl N.	21	"	"
325	Booth, Sydney S. Rev.	35	Clergyman	England
335	Sanderson, Frank L.	39	Watchmaker	20 Moraine st.
337	Stewart, Thomas	29	Electrician	325 Trapelo road
339	Oken, Severin	43	Organ builder	same
339	Comey, Karl S.	33	Salesman	"
341	Shaughnessy, John J.	38	Clerk	"
347	Farrell, Albert L.	31	Note broker	"
347	Stackhouse, Hartley	36	Shipper	California
349	McLearn, Arthur H.	39	Lawyer	Watertown
361	Glaser, Frank	68	Retired	same
365	Virchow, Albert G.	54	Store-keeper	"
365	Virchow, Carl F.	22	Clerk	"
365	McAleer, Thomas G.	55	Orderly	Somerville
365	McAleer, Dearborn J.	22	Pressman	"
365	Morrill, Chas. H.	26	Tile-layer	So. Boston
365	Morrill, Winfred	31	Engineer	" "
403	Magnuson, Bror E.	29	Engraver	same
403	Potter, William A.	31	Clerk	"
403	Lynch, Walter H.	20	Florist	"
403	Lynch, Elwood N.	29	"	
403	Lynch, Norman R.	59	Caretaker	
407	McNamee, David I.	56	Retired	
407	McNamee, John R.	23	Electrician	
431	Preston, J. Stanley	57	Vocal teacher	
431	Preston, William A.	25	Chiropodist	
435	Williams, George A.	46	Garage	
435	Williams, Salisbury H.	75	Retired	
437	Bartlett, George O.	37	Dentist	"
439	Wellsman, J. Fred	35	Lineman	616 Trapelo road
439	Wellsman, George A.	23	"	16 Church st.
489	Sullivan, Stephen F.	39	Foreman	same
489	Mamelian, Paul	52	Pressman	Cambridge
541	Farmer, John	72	Retired	N. Y.
	Cochran, Myron J.	48	Nurse	same
	Hines, Thomas R.	56	Painter	"
628	Douglas, William H.	47	Draughtsman	"
622	Parks, Geo. W.	48	Police officer	
622	Parks, Wm. A.	21	Bookkeeper	
616	McLaskey, Miles	35	Salesman	"
614	Simm, Alva G.	24	Insurance	606 Trapelo road
612	Castner, Eldorus A.	55	Weigher	same
610	McConnell, Chas. W.	29	Salesman	Concord Jct.
610	Lawrence, Alden L.	39	Shoe maker	Pepperill
606	Daly Thomas A.	37	Engineer	Watertown
600	Gowan, Alonzo	41	"	same
596	Flett, Geo. C.	55	Superintendent	"
596	Flett, J. Watson	22	Student	"
592	Crawford, Alex.	49	Foreman	48 Church st.

TRAPELO ROAD, - Continued.

No.	Name.	Age.	Occupation.	Residence 1914.
590	Joy, Daniel A.	28	Instructor	same
588	Hoyer, Ernest	44	Nurse	"
586	Troy, Martin	61	Foreman	"
586	Troy, John E.	25	Civil engineer	
580	Simm, William J.	60	Engineer	
580	Robinson, Vernon C.	32	Salesman	
578	Wolff, Louis J.	62	Chef	
574	Powell, John R.	22	Engineer	
574	Simm, Wilbert E.	38	State inspector	
570	Logan, James R.	49	Master mechanic	"
566	Smith, Horace C.	37	Supervisor	McLean Hosp.
562	Brown, Edward Jr.	62	Commission merchant	same
562	Goss, George F.	40	Clerk	"
548	Cunningham, Michael E.	25	Station agent	"
548	Tucker, Edward P.	71	Retired	
546	Foote, Henry S.	78	"	
544	Cochrane, Alexander Y.	66	Carpenter	"
438	Page, George A.	68	Retired	23 Waverley st.
438	Stevens, Walter, L. Jr.	31	Garage	same
430	Wentzel, Philip	55	Grocer	"
426	Troccoli, Achille	35	Barber	"
426	Elder, Chas.	40	Chauffeur	
426	Dunn, Winfield T.	31	Salesman	
422	Camack, David	25	Machinist	"
422	Camack, William	30	Piano maker	same
422	Bickford, Edwin D.	49	Watchmaker	"
416	Bird, Frank J.	25	Cable-splicer	24 Thomas st.
416	Fitz, Norman E.	36	Driver	Everett
416	Anderson, Axel D.	44	Laundryman	same
410	Courtney, Daniel J.	45	Machinist	Wilson ave.
410	Jaynes, James	38	Clerk	same
410	Crocker, Geo. R.	52	House painter	"
408	Burrell, Chas. A.	27	Buyer	Revere
408	Ginesti, Dominic	47	Real estate	same
400	Hall, Harrison B.	75	Retired	"
346	Boyd, James V.	37	Pen maker	"
346	Mack, Fred F.	30	Fruit merchant	
346	McNeil, Edmund J.	43	Physician	
242	McCarthy, J. V.	50	Real estate	
146	Horne, Richard B.	42	Market gardener	
146	Hayes, William	40	Farmer	"

VINCENT AVENUE.

5	Busky, Fred H.	25	School teacher	Roxbury
7	Foster, David H.	37	Bookkeeper	113 White st.
7	Goodwin, Harry	22	"	Everett
9	Muirhead, James	42	Builder	same
15	Rodd, Irving E.	22	Carpenter	"
15	Rodd, Chas. H.	46	"	"

WALNUT STREET.

No.	Name.	Age.	Occupation.	Residence 1914.
11	Culici, Nino	25	Farm hand	Beech st.
11	Culici, Joseph	32	" "	" "
11	Arno, Paul	22	" "	" "
11	Culici, Paul	27	" "	" "
11	Travaglio, Frank	42	Laborer	same
15	Paone, Gaetano	28	Fruit dealer	"
15	Angelo, Michael	35	Laborer	"
65	Arno, Giovanni	50	Farm hand	Watertown
65	Arno, Joseph	25	Barber	"
65	Arno, Nino	22	Farm hand	"
65	Levao, Nino	25	" "	5 B street
65	Cucinotta, Giovanni	34	Carpenter	same
79	Smith, Wm. J.	49	Electrician	Cambridge
85	Briggs, Clarence V.	24	Elevator operator	51 White st.
85	Briggs, Frank B.	21	"	"
85	Briggs, James H.	50	Cabinet maker	"
87	Wilson, Frank	52	Painter	same
87	Wilson, Thomas	26	Watchmaker	"
40	Buonfiglio, Tony	36	Fruit dealer	"
	Connell, James W.	28	Mechanic	"
	Little, Richard	32	Ivory cutter	46 Myrtle st.

WAVERLEY STREET.

No.	Name.	Age.	Occupation.	Residence 1914.
23	Epps, Frederick H.		Salesman	Winthrop
23	Stowe, Clarence G.	42	"	same
35	Poor, Fred	42	Manager	"
37	Corbett, Alexander E.	35	Druggist	"
41	Raymond, Warren S.	24	Organ builder	Plymouth
41	Clisby, John P.	73	Painter	Somerville
41	Bridgham, Percy A.		Lawyer	"
55	Davis Ralph S.	40	Clerk	same
61	Locke Frank M.	33	"	"
61	Alger Frank W.	24	"	"
61	Leacy Martin	37	Teamster	"
61	Tracy, Maurice L.	21	Clerk	Vermont
61	Alger, James H.	60	Teamster	same
61	Alger, Ernest E.	22	Clerk	"
61	Benoit, Jesse O.	35	Salesman	"
69	Miller, John F.	48	Clerk	
69	Miller, James	80	Retired	
75	Webster, Daniel P.	45	Carpenter	
75	Webster, Henry E.	22	Bookkeeper	
115	Miller, Joseph A.	64	Cabinet maker	
125	Stuart, William A.	40	Furniture mover	
125	Wildes, Charles H.	77	Retired	
149	Murphy Frank E.	31	Bookkeeper	
149	Murphy Thomas W.	62	Laborer	
	Broderick John F.	46	Motorman	

WAVERLEY STREET, - Continued.

No.	Name.	Age.	Occupation.	Residence 1914.
206	Brown, Edward	32	Expressman	same
202	McDonald, James J.	38	Letter carrier	"
200	Cleland, Frank	48	Retired	"
200	Toomey, Timothy F.	32	Letter carrier	
198	Higgins, Bernard	45	Gardener	
194	Quigley, James	60	Laborer	
194	Griffin, Timothy	24	Plumber	
194	Tolland, Daniel	50	Gardener	
194	Cummings, John	25	Laborer	
194	Fallon, Matthew	37	"	
188	Niland, Martin	46	Gardener	
182	Schultz, Rudolf	36	Fireman	"
180	Cronin, John	40	Clerk	Watertown
178	Johnson, Emil	34	Laborer	"
176	Donovan, Dennis	35	"	same
176	Crine, Wm.	32	"	"
172	Murphy, Daniel J.	44	"	"
168	Elias, Joseph	45	Salesman	
156	Connors, John	45	Laborer	
146	Ingram, Lester W.	44	Lawyer	
142	Edmonstone, Wm. E.	26	Teacher	
142	Kennedy, John A.	39	Salesman	
138	Neptune, Richard	50	Engineer	
138	Avery, Niram	76	Retired	
130	Robinson, Geo. E.	26	Draughtsman	
130	Willard, Frank H.	39	Salesman	
122	Melanson, Chas.	21	Student	
122	Melanson, Delby C.	47	Carpenter	
122	Melanson, Theodore J.	49	"	
112	Warren, Chas.	38	Clerk	
112	Connelly, Dennis F.	30	"	
106	Savinano, James	39	Teamster	
104	Lomeyers, Joseph	35	Laborer	
104	Grieano, Nicholas	34	"	
74	Sullivan, Patrick	45		
70	Dow, Oscar W.	41	Manager	
68	Austin, Newell B.	46	Conductor	
64	Shedd, A. Lincoln	48	Inspector	
52	Taylor, John	57	Expressman	
52	Taylor, Wm.	25	"	"
50	Heckman, Raymond H.	37	Engineer	Dorchester
48	Barnes, Harry T.	31	Bank teller	same
46	Sparrow, Wendell H.	55	Contractor	151 Lexington st.
44	Hathaway, LeRoy	33	Manager	same
40	Stevens, Henry M.	67	Electrician	Roxbury
40	Stevens, Edward H.	43	"	"
22	Houlahan Chas. H.	65	Town Clerk	same
10	Barker, Albert H.	41	Clerk	"

WHITCOMB STREET.

No.	Name.	Age.	Occupation.	Residence 1914
11	Pierce, Harry W.	33	Asst. manager	same
15	Serverance, George A.	45	Trav. salesman	Penn.
21	Putney, George A.	52	Foreman	same
22	Cooksley, Alfred	39	Manager	W. Roxbury
22	Cooksley, Daniel	76	Retired	" "
20	Gordon, Albert B.	26	Clerk	same
20	Gordon, George K.	27	"	"

WHITE STREET.

No.	Name.	Age.	Occupation.	Residence 1914
51	Jenks, Simeon	64	Carpenter	same
51	Flewelling, Fred	46	Engineer	Cambridge
	Mahoney, Wm. F.	50	Barber	same
67	McCarthy, Charles E.	40	Grocer	"
113	Harvey, Wendell T.	22	Clerk	Boston
113	Wright, Willis F.	44	Driver	19 Concord ave.
113	Ripley, Leonard F.	63	Retired	175 White st.
113	Ripley, Harry M.	38	Real estate & Insurance	" " "
117	Goodwin, Elisha	46	Manager	same
125	Hale, Charles E.	53	"	"
125	Hale, Brownell	22	Clerk	"
175	Reed, Chas. C.	30	Paymaster	70 White st.
185	Latimer, Hugh	30	Collector	Newton
189	Ripley, Orville	74	Patern maker	same
213	Handrahan, Raymond A.	33	Machinist	Waltham
215	Perkins, Wilfred D.	35	"	Cambridge
217	Daly, John F.	35	Insurance	same
223	Beebe, Maxwell N.	34	Cashier	"
223	Beebe, Manley C.	32	Draughtsman	"
223	King, Melvin E.	69	Clergyman	
225	Strum, Clarence E.	44	Contractor	
227	Hamm, John D.	42	"	
227	Munn, Eugene E.	30	Salesman	
229	Munday, Willard E.	32	Clerk	
231	Smith, Fred A.	29	Treasurer	
231	Stankard, John J.	37	Bookkeeper	
242	Morash, Chas. E.	58	Builder	
238	Clement, William	38	Salesman	
236	Morash, C. Ross	25	Builder	
234	Carter, Chester H.	36	Engineer	
232	Briggs, Benjamin F.	42	Manager	
230	Libby, Joseph E.	47	Clerk	
230	Pollock, Leland W.	29	Lawyer	
220	Ross, Wilbert A.	33	Milk dealer	"
220	Young, Henry	30	Driver	Waltham
214	Reed, Albert F.	30	Teacher	Waverley st.
214	Banks, Amos L.	55	Retired	same
208	Hinckley, Crandall H.	35	Merchant	"
208	Cherry, Willard E.	33	Real estate & Insurance	same
168	Taylor, Edwin P.	51	Superintendent	"

WHITE STREET, - Continued.

No.	Name.	Age.	Occupation.	Residence 1914.
158	Stowe, Carle	39	Actor	Brookline
)ff	Bisnaw, George A.	54	Carpenter	158 White st.
)ff	Angell, Ernest F.	31	Jobber	" " "
140	Anastas, Panos	23	Clerk	same
140	Cokinos, Nicholas J.	35	Fruit dealer	"
140	Desillve, Joseph	45	Laborer	"
140	Gerace, Frank	34	"	"
140	Anastas, Peter	26	Grocer	New York
240	Cokinos, Geo.	24	Waiter	same
140	Fulginiti, Dominico	45	Expressman	"
132	Young, Ulysses S.	45	Treasurer	"
132	Jameson, Claude S.	29	Gen. manager	
120	Bradbury, John P.	57	Purveyor	"
114	Webber, Walter L.	42	Fire chief	Dorchester
114	Loring, Joshua	55	Importer	same
114	Loring, Bentley E.	28	Salesman	"
100	Garrity, Geo. A.	27	Electrician	"
100	George, Edwin R.	87	Retired	
100	Lothrop, James F.	37	Foreman	
100	Warren, Orvis A.	34	C6nductor	"
70	Terry, Orrin A.	30	Golf instructor	New Jersey
62	Richardson, William B.	45	Clerk	same
62	Devany, Patrick A.	35	Physician	"
50	Carroll, Wm. H.	22	Asst. station agent	"
50	Carroll, Thomas	48	Teamster	

WILSON AVENUE.

No.	Name.	Age.	Occupation.	Residence 1914.
5	True, John	59	Packer	same
25	Freeman, Wm. H.	22	Conductor	"
25	Linscott, Robert N.	29	Clerk	"
25	Smith, Austin C.	38	Mechanic	"
29	Haviland, Wm. J.	27	Tel. inspector	Cambridge
29	Kellogg, Arthur J.	38	Watchmaker	Waltham
29	Mead, F. Walton Jr.	22	Carpenter	Hingham
33	Hennessy, James F.	41	Clerk	same
33	Fitzgerald, Edward G.	41	Conductor	52 Marlboro st.
37	Mullett, Fred A.	38	Clerk	85 Concord ave.
37	True, Ross	44	Salesman	same
37	Harrington, John J.	33	Machinist	Cambridge
44	Melville, Samuel P.	28	Engineer	same
42	Patterson, William H.	38	"	"
34	McKay, Robert F.	35	Salesman	"
32	Vine, Franklin H.	36	Manager	
26	Costello, Michael	38	Fireman	
24	Bromley, Samuel J.	37	Carpenter	
20	Ferguson, Robert R.	29	Mason	"
20	Gigger, Emory W.	34	Engineer	McLean Hosp.
20	Brown, John O.	29	Carpenter	Cambridge
4	Teed, William E.	28	Chauffeur	20 Wilson ave.

WINTER STREET.

No.	Name.	Age.	Occupation.	Residence 1914.
	Smith, Chas. E.	55	Farmer	same
	Kendall, Arthur E.	37	"	"

WOODLAND STREET.

No.	Name.	Age.	Occupation.	Residence 1914.
15	Guertin, Augustus	34	Auto repairer	Boston
15	Dugan, Peter A.	32	Shipper	same
15	Dugan, Charles F.	35	Superintendent	"
15	Dugan, Peter	69	Retired	"
15	Curtin, William W.	21	Clerk	Boston
15	Millette, Francis L.	29	Bookkeeper	"
17	Quigley, Patrick	45	Laborer	same
12	Maguire, James J.	31	Salesman	"
12	Clunan, Patrick J.	31	Laborer	"

NOTE.--The word "same" refers to the street of last year's residence, the number not always being the same.

PRECINCT 3.

BELMONT STREET.

No.	Name.	Age.	Occupation.	Residence 1914
113	Cummings, Richard J. J.	58	Printer	Medford
113	Cummings, Charles H.	46	"	same
117	McCarthy, Edward H.	35	Railroading	"
117	Sullivan, John	68	Retired	"
121	Galvin, Mortimer	40	Florist	
121	Galvin, John	35	Insurance	
125	Feeney, Patrick J.	45	Steamfitter	
125	Feeney, Joseph P.	24		
127	Sullivan, John F.	36	Postal clerk	"
137	Gallagher, Hughie	65	Packer	Watertown
139	Beardsley, Crowell E.	54	Teamster	Cambridge
143	Mullen, Arthur J.	23	Rubber worker	Watertown
143	Gardner, James	50	Janitor	"
145	Vickberg, Abel	42	Painter	Cambridge
145	Lamont, Raymond	25	Insurance	same
163	Turk, Frank W.	32	Trav. salesman	"
163	McIntosh, Walter H.	26	Bookkeeper	Somerville
163	Tippett, Thomas M.	55	Repairman	Cambridge
171	Rose, Louis E.	63	Market gardener	same
175	Cunningham, Dr. E. A.	34	Physician	183 Belmont st.
175	Arrington, Arthur W.	39	Bookkeeper	same
177	Douthart, R. S.	31	Chemist	"
177	Vaughan, F. W.	60	Foreman	"
179	Jarvis, Charles A.	45	Printer	
179	Cherry, Arthur B.	28	Salesman	"
179	Gould, Ernest L.	34	Superintendent	Boston
181	Lamson, Howard E.	26	Tailor	same
183	Norwood, Roscoe	65	Grocer	Cambridge
211	Hood, James H.	32	Civil engineer	same
215	Hunt, Fred O.	34	Mail clerk	Boston
215	Cooper, A. H.	29	Civil engineer	Watertown
215	Blair, James A.	40	Electrotype finisher	same
219	Lee, Walter N.	45	Salesman	"
221	Loomer, Ashley	35	Hardware	
223	Knudsin, Axel E.	41	Cigarmaker	
223	Kilburn, Austin S.	50	Photogapher	
225	Duplessis, Nelson K.	44	Com. photographer	
229	Garfield, Walter T.	33	Physician	
229	Foster, Lewis W.	28	Architect	"
229	Baker, Cassius H.	24	Clerk	Lynn
229	Herrick, Robert W.	28	Salesman	same
229	Reilly, Russell G.	33	Manager	"
231	Henshaw, Charles S.	39	Automobiles	
235	Burrage, Paul	30	Insurance	21 Falmouth st.

BELMONT STREET, - Continued.

No.	Name.	Age.	Occupation.	Residence 1914.
235	Hull, Chester A.	34	Druggist	same
307	Mulrey, Patrick	37	Chauffeur	"
315	Stults, John V. N.	77	Retired	"
315	McCreary, Lewis S.	42	Merchant	"
395	Hanson, Wm. C.	40	Physician	Cambridge
397	LaFlamme, T. Leo	40	Dentist	"
399	Warwick, George W.	64	Treasurer	same
423	Fuller, Alfred C.	52	Real estate	"
491	Greer, Thomas A.	34	Superintendent	Cambridge
491	O'Neil, Thomas H.	28	Newspaper work	Danvers
545	Payson, Gilbert R.	46	Wharfinger	same

BERWICK STREET.

No.	Name.	Age.	Occupation.	Residence 1914.
51	Burns, Edward F. P.	36	Salesman	same
51	Conant, Chas. B.	75	Real estate	Cambridge
51	Frehrickson, Fritz W.	39	Carpenter	same
55	Farwell, Edward C.	28	Machinist	"
55	Levitt, Harry W.	28	Chauffeur	Cambridge
55	Pittenger, Charles	24	Mechanic	"
57	Hill, William M.	57	Accountant	Revere
57	Brassil, Thomas J.	42	Real estate	same
59	Malmsten, Ernest A.	35	Piano polisher	"
59	Lee, S. Southard	28	Machinist	"
59	Mahegan, Albert F.	40	Florist	"
63	Walker, Charles H.	26	Traveling freight agt.	20 Moraine st.
63	Sanborn, C. Francis	37	Salesman	same
67	Emerson, George C.	31	"	New York
67	Follett, Leslie C.	33	Bookkeeper	same
67	Blood, Wallace S.	34	Auto business	4 Worcester st.
69	Bushway, James H.	28	Merchant	same
64	Stover, Elroy S.	38	Salesman	Somerville
62	Steeves, Everett W.	31	Contractor	"
56	Delany, Edmund H.	48	Photographer	same
56	Dunnell, James A.	68	Artesian wells	"
56	Dunnell, Harry R.	24	Clerk	"
56	Robbins, Raymond L.	30	Printer	

COMMON STREET.

No.	Name.	Age.	Occupation.	Residence 1914.
492	Olsson, Frederic A.	45	Art store	same
492	Temple, Edward H.	35	Instructor	"
	Peede, T. Richard	51	Clergyman	"
	Peede, Loring G.	22	Salesman	"
440	Brown, John H.	45	Treasurer	Brookline
440A	Reynolds, Percy I.	29	Salesman	Allston
442	Parks, Edward E.	33	Sales manager	N. H.
410	Ellison, Wm. H.	55	Retired	same

COMMON STREET, - Continued.

No.	Name.	Age.	Occupation.	Residence 1914.
386	Poole, William H.	51	Piano manufacturer	same
386	Poole, Ava	23	Manager	"

CUSHING AVENUE.

No.	Name.	Age.	Occupation.	Residence 1914.
27	Hilton, Everett S.	47	Merchant	same
53	Locke, Galen L.	21	Bookkeeper	"
53	Locke, George S.	48	Pattern maker	"
53	Locke, Melvin	20	Bookkeeper	
59	Locke, William H.	74	Piano regulator	
80	Crowell, William F.	46	Traffic manager	
46	Smith, Fred L.	70	Real estate	
34	Kedian, James E.	45	Grocer	
26	Vollintine, Thomas	75	Clerk	
26	Vollintine, Chas. H. Jr.	40	Chauffeur	
26	Vollintine, Chas. H.	68	Retired	
20	Hilton, John P.	40	Clerk	
20	Hilton, Frank H.	38	Manager	

DARTMOUTH STREET.

No.	Name.	Age.	Occupation.	Residence 1914.
45	Alput, Julius S.	35	Merchant	Dorchester
45	Fuller, Ralph E.	23	Bookkeeper	Newton
53	Morgan, John C.	41	Auto business	same
53A	Livermore, Charles E.	39	Biologist	"
55	Baxter, Frank W.	33	Foreman	"
55	Beatson, Jesse W.	42	Secretary	
55	Glading, Wilson	28	Salesman	
61	Mera, William A.	30	"	
61	Erickson, John C.	23	Machinist	
61	Erickson, Arvid	24	Piano tuner	
61	Erickson, John	53	Machinist	"
61	MacLane, Vinal B.	34	Driver	Cambridge
81	Andrews, Melvin C.	31	Milk business	same
81	Walsh, Edward E.	36	Cable splicer	"
68	Fillmore, John M.	31	Carpenter	"
68	Hedlund, True	46	Chef	
66	Johnson, Allan	33	Carpenter	"
64	Seaberg, Harry	22	Machinist	Hyde Park
64	Carlson, Robert	35	Carpenter	same
58	Cobb, Howard P.	29	Engineer	"
58	Morse, Floyd B.	39	Insurance	"
58	Parry, Chas. G.	59	Demonstrator	
58	Probert, Albert A.	29	Concrete inspector	
56	Steele, Augustine J.	39	Tailor	"
56	Rich, Robert R.	24	Dentist	Boston
56	Blomquist, Olof	41	Painter	"
54	McIlroy, John	45	Plumbing & Heating	same

DARTMOUTH STREET, - Continued.

No.		Age.	Occupation.	Residence 1914.
52	Lambie, George	30	Plumber	same
52	Maineau, Nelson	30	Machinist	"
50	MacLennan, John	41	Master plumber	"
48	Johnson, Augustus B.	35	Supt.	"
44	Dakin, George H.	45	Salesman	Boston

ELM STREET.

7	Cook, Joseph E.	46	Contractor	same
7	Cook, Charles W.	26	Salesman	"
7	Cook, Joseph E. Jr.	23	Clerk	"
7	Gray, James	38	Printer	
9	Kirschten Frederick W.	47	Foreman	"
9	Cooper, Frederick J.	27	Granit carver	Maine
9	Cooper, Sidney F.	55	" "	same
22	Rockett, John W.	35	Fish and Meat Dealer	Chelsea
22	Reynolds, Michael B.	33	Foreman	same
22	Marsh, Ernest V.	32	Musician	"
20	Johnson, Axel	45	Steward	"
20	Baker, Taylor	30	Draughtsman	"
20	Lundberg, Wm. A.	25	Postal clerk	Roxbury
16	Lindstrom, Frank O.	50	Mechanic	same
16	Stevens, Fred	35	Salesman	"
16	Rich, Samuel T.	24	Rubber work	"
12	Bailey, Fred	45	Printer	
10	Lonergan, James M.	46	Iron moulder	
10	Lonergan, Frank E.	23	Printer	
6	Larrabee, Bertram C.	31	Instructor	
6	Farmer, Geo. T.	40	Engineer	
6	Dimick, Jos. H.	30	Insurance	

EXETER STREET.

5	Chausey, Maxime E.	40	Brakeman	Watertown
7	Garland, Charles A.	51	Agent	same
9	Exeter, Frederick J.	29	Wholesale confectioner	12 Marion road
15	Nelson, Carl E.	60	Retired	same
15	Miller, Walter J.	31	Buyer	"
15	Ordway, Walter M.	60	Manager	"
17	McNealy, Francis	34	Cutter	
19	Splaine, Richard H.	34	Claim agent	
22	Krause, Herman H.	45	Steel engraver	

EXETER STREET, - Continued.

No.	Name.	Age.	Occupation.	Residence 1914.
20	Pugh, William J.	55	Foreman	same
16	Robinson, Walter H.	39	Manufacturer	"
12	Rose, Peter A.	50	Inspector	"
4	Anderson, John	30	Metal worker	Walnut st.
2	Hines, Bartley	35	Printer	same

FAIRVIEW AVENUE.

No.	Name.	Age.	Occupation.	Residence 1914.
21	Mason, Alban A.	63	Machinist	same
21	Mason, Nathaniel J.	26	Mason	Boston
23	Skahan, John J.	50	Gardener	same
63	Norton, James E.	38	Market Gardener	"
65	Schaab, Philip A.	30	Bookkeeper	"
87	Corcoran, John F.	39	Fireman	
87	Corcoran, Michael J.	76	Retired	

FALMOUTH STREET.

No.	Name.	Age.	Occupation.	Residence 1914.
3	Johnson, Olof	43	Builder	same
5	Kenny, John	44	Boilermaker	"
9	Coe, John W.	44	Machinist	"
15	Morse, John	50	Lunch room	
17	Roper, Chas. H.	36	Asst. supt.	"
17	Spear, Alonzo P.	50	Rubber worker	Maine
21	MacLean, Archibald	50	Supt.	same
21	Perrault, James E.	39	Rubber worker	"
25	Pease, Alexander	70	Retired	Cambridge
25	Hall, Harry	25	Salesman	"
25	Mackenzie, Fredwith R.	32	Lawyer	same
25	Coombs, Martin A.	40	Engineer	"
25	Ellsworth, Henry E.	28	Chemist	Boston
25	Ewell, Thomas B.	83	Retired	same
29	Jones, Lewis A.	34	Lawyer	"
29	Holmburg, John	70	Retired	"
31	Brooks, Geo. F. T.	44	Purchasing agt.	
35	Weston, Ernest	24	Chauffeur	
35	Weston, Louis F.	55	Printer	
56	Fitch, Wilbur R.	35	Designing engr.	
50	Murray, John D.	35	Foreman	
48	Bailey, Howard C.	32	Salesman	
42	Fletcher, Richmond K.	30	Architect	
42	Piper, Fred E. R.	30	Insurance	
42	Cuffs, James A.	46	Custom House examiner	"
40	Reynolds, J. L.	43	Commercial trav.	25 Falmouth st.
38	Stevens, Herbert A.	27	Electrical engr.	33 Marion road
34	Almgren, George W.	41	Carpenter	same
34	Rote, Charles C.	56	Salesman	"

FALMOUTH STREET, - Continued.

No.	Name.	Age.	Occupation.	Residence 1914.
34	Rote, Donald I.	23	Electrician	same
30	Scotton, Alfred E.	42	Organ builder	"
30	Crawford, Arthur A.	33	Dentist	"
24	O'Neil, Michael	44	Insurance	"
24	Johnson, Daniel C.	26	Cutter	Watertown
24	Johnson, Carl W.	33	Foreman	same
22	King, Arthur J.	40	Dry goods	"
18	Russell, Ralph P.	36	Purchasing agt.	"
12	Berger, Kenneth	39	Manager	Rhode Island
10	Taylor, Albert B.	29	Salesman	So. Boston

GROVE STREET.

No.	Name.	Age.	Occupation.	Residence 1914.
33	Gallagher, William A.	40	Buyer	Boston
33	Gallagher, John	35	Laborer	"
33	Gallagher, William	72	Retired	"
33	Gildea, James	74	"	same
37	Tiernay, Thomas J.	47	Marble cutter	"
37	Brennan, James E.	32	Supt.	Somerville
37	Specht, K. E.	32	Engineer	same
57	King, Charles M.	33	P. O. clerk	"
59	Hellen, John	42	Grocer	"
57	Doyle, Frederick L.	33	Liquor business	
61	Silva, John P.	48	Cabinet maker	"
61	Martinolich, Nicholas	34	Engineer	Cambridge
61	Harrington, James	36	Iron moulder	same
65	Smith, Patrick J.	38	Foreman	23 Park road
65	Fogg, Alton T.	36	Automobile business	same
65	Cosgrove, James W.	46	Conductor	"
69	Roberts, David R.	63	Roofer	"
69	Roberts, David R. Jr.	33	Carpenter	"
69	Peterson, John	26	Chemist	Cambridge
69	Gray, Joseph M.	32	Salesman	same
73	Twomey, George H.	33	"	"
73	Kelly, John J.	40	Motorman	"
73	Campbell, Walter	32	Rubber worker	"
87	Dorney, John T.	20	Salesman	Revere
87	Courtney, Wm. J.	72	Retired	same
87	Christiansen, Norman	22	Salesman	Wilmington
87	Powers, Frank L.	25	Asst. foreman	same
89	McNamee, Wm. A.	54	Police officer	"
89	McNamee, A. Percy	20	Student	"
91	Skahan, Edward F.	50	Market gardener	
95	McKeen, Leslie R.	45	Salesman	
106	Ware, Leslie A.	40	Wood worker	
98	Grellish, Patrick	49	Teamster	
74	Skahan, John W.	56	Market gardener	
52	Shirley, James F.	45	Mechanic	"
50	Parsons, Herbert E.	35	Supt.	145 Belmont st.

GROVE STREET, - Continued.

No.	Name.	Age.	Occupation.	Residence 1914.
48	Longden, Joseph	20	Steamfitter	same
46	Barry, Michael J.	46	Bookbinder	"
44	Bugney, Walter K.	34	Rubber worker	Watertown
42	Johnson, John	40	" "	same
40	Elertson, Emil	58	Painter	27 Park road
40	Olson, Alvin G.	30	Electrician	" " "
38	Carey, Harry	28	Police officer	same
36	McCutcheon, James E.	38	Blacksmith	"
32	Rogers, James F.	32	Machinist	17 Park road
30	Hankin, Chas. A.	30	Clerk	same
28	Long, Jer. J.	60	Retired	"
28	Long, James F.	21	Druggist	"
28	Long, Edward	26	Bookbinder	

HILLSIDE TERRACE.

No.	Name.	Age.	Occupation.	Residence 1914.
21	Merrill, Allyne L.	50	Teacher	same
35	Johnston, William A.	46	Professor	"
20	Lister, Robert N.	50	Vocal teacher	"
20	Richmond, Harold E.	30	Designer	Adams
10	French, Wm. C.	40	Bus. manager	same
	Bates, Fred O.	45	Salesman	"
	Cutler, George H.	53	Hardware	Arlington
	James, William H.	37	Rendering	same

LAWNDALE STREET.

No.	Name.	Age.	Occupation.	Residence 1914.
15	Churchill, Gilman	28	President	same
15	Preble, George E.	38	Furniture salesman	"
17	Hollander, Wilkie B.	30	Salesman	Brookline
17	Wellman, Walter F.	35	"	Cambridge
17	Wellman, Geo. F.	66	Clerk	"
19	Dillon, Edwin S.	38	Wholesale fruit	same
19	Dillon, Stephen N.	24	Bookkeeper	"
21	Hutchinson, James	60	Salesman	"
52	Jameson, Winthrop S.	40	Auto supplies	Cambridge
	Beetle, Leslie V.	24	Salesman	same
	Beetle, W. F.	57	Merchant	"

LINDEN AVENUE.

No.	Name.	Age.	Occupation.	Residence 1914.
	Drew, Ernest L.	33	Insurance	Boston

MARION ROAD.

No.	Name.	Age.	Occupation.	Residence 1914.
1	Johnson, Carl	31	Piano Maker	same

MARION ROAD, - Continued.

No.	Name.	Age.	Occupation.	Residence 1914.
3	Powers, Leslie M.	35	Clerk	same
3	Westlund, Gustaf	34	Piano maker	"
5	Waterman, Wm. F.	28	Upholsterer	Stoneham
7	Dickinson, Eben C.	21	Salesman	same
7	Finnegan, Thos.	35	Inspector	"
9	Hamblen, Clarence	33	Furniture mover	"
11	Arnoldson, Frank	45	Painter	
11	Fisher, Frank	24	Plumber	
13	Werge, John A.	46	Engineer	
15	Anderson, Gustof	37	Clerk	
15	Kuhn, David P.	55	Grocer	
17	Brown, Bertram L.	30	Cashier	"
19	Banfil, Jerrold W.	26	Foreman	No. Sudbury
21	Waid, John F.	39	Manufacturer	same
23	Almgren, Axel	43	Butcher	"
25	Svensson, Lars A.	28	Painter	
25	Grey, Bernard C.	26	Manager and salesman	Boston
25	Hill, Edward E.	22	Broker	"
27	Perry, Ernest	35	Tel. manager	same
29	Smith, Owen J.	40	Piano maker	"
31	Baldwin, Walter F.	41	Merchant	"
33	Bennett, John K.	33	Stage manager	
35	Bushby, Warren	54	Machinist	same
35	Ward, Ralph C.	25	Clerk	Cambridge
37	Jones, George H.	32	Machinist	same
39	Shaw, Walter J.	30	Salesman	"
39	Pretat, Charles J.	26	Electrician	"
43	Culhane, Daniel	21	Printer	
45	Johnston, Albert H.	28	Salesman	
47	Wiley, Arthur M.	28	Insurance broker	"
47	Towle, Herbert C.	25	Secretary	Cambridge
49	Macgregor, Daniel	41	Carpenter	same
51	Rollins, Harold E.	26	Statistician	1 Orchard st..
51	Fanning, John F.	35	Buyer	same
26	Tufts, Royal G.	25	Clerk	"
26	Henley, Joseph A.	30	Manager	Waltham
24	Ross, R. N.	31	Clerk	same
22	Angell, James G.	32	Moulder	"
22	Latimer, Elbert S.	32	Salesman	"
20	Syversen, S.	36	Carpenter	Cambridge
18	Lockhart, Edward C.	52	Asst. supt.	same
18	Wood, George D.	54	Book seller	"
16	Fletcher, H. L.	40	Asst. treas.	"
14	Perry, Stanley R.	30	Clerk	
12	Whittemore, Casper M.	30	"	
10	Fowler. C. R.	35	Salesman	"
8	Catton, W. R.	29	Teacher	62 Marlboro st.
4	Gethro, George W.	20	Clerk	No. Carolina
4	Brown, Thomas R.	30	"	same
2	Stiansen, Axel H.	50	Draughtsman	"

MARLBORO STREET.

Occupation.

9	Turk, Jos. M.	58	Station master	same
15	Bear, John R.	23	Insurance	"
15	Cummings, Chas. F.	55	Printer	"
15	Joyce, Wm. H.	37	Machinist	
17	Nelson, Olof	46	"	
19	Reynolds, Wm.	50	"	
33	Porter, Wm. M.	50	Restaurant	
33	Bent, Maurice	26	Carpenter	"
37	White, D. Winthrop	30	Salesman	Watertown
37	Erstby, Gothard	20	Helper	same
37	Weeks, Cyrus	54	Manufacturer	"
41	Olson, Edward	53	Grocer	"
43	Lawson, Hans L.	37	Carpenter	
45	Egelin, Ernest	45	Painter	
45	Johnson, Frank W.	28	Designer	
45	Malmsten, Chas.	40	Piano polisher	
49	Magnuson, Eric	30	Engineer	
49	Danforth, Wm. J.	35	Druggist	
57	Fuller, Frank	38	Clerk	
57	Emerson, Chas.	72	Retired	
57	Westby, Peter	41	Janitor	
61	Hollis, John T.	30	Printer	
61	Lamson, Henry H.	50	Teamster	
61	Gardener, Alfred H.	34	Printer	
65	Lewis, Ellsworth M.	50	Engineer	
65	Roslund, John	47	Glass cutter	
69	Caulfield, George	43	Broker	
69	Olive, Chas.	40	Clerk	"
69	Benson, Carl	27	Piano worker	Waltham
73	Johnson Carl E.	26	Printer	same
73	Pearce, Aleck	43	Machinist	"
73	Bliss, Franklin H.	52	Optician	"
75	Moody, Ralph L.	42	Supt.	
75	Baxter, Herbert L.	27	Foreman	
75	Kihlberg, Karl A.	74	Retired	"
77	Sandborg, F. W.	27	Machinist	Cambridge
77	Svenson, E.	28	"	56 Dartmouth st.
79	Weeks, Harold E.	24	Grocer	same
79	Weeks, Bedford H.	53	"	
62	Bradley, James J.	39	P. O. clerk	77 Marlboro st.
62	Macdonald, John J.	38	Printer	Watertown
62	Clausen, Peter W.	54	Machinist	same
62	Clausen, Holger W.	26	Civil engineer	"
58	Nickerson, Edrick R.	32	Salesman	"
58	Nickerson, Geo. E.	33	"	
58	Johnson, George	53	Special police	
58	Roper, John M.	49	Foreman	
56	Hawkes, Nathan	33	Asst. manager	
56	Stearns, Sherman	39	Salesman	
54	Schultz, William C.	34	"	

MARLBORO STREET, - Continued.

No.	Name.	Age.	Occupation.	Residence 1914.
54	Daly, John	35	Engineer	same
54	McDonald, Thomas H.	34	Druggist	"
52	Terrio Simon H.	48	Fish dealer	"
52	Hawkes, A. J.	54	Instructor	"
52	Morgan, Otto F.	27	Clerk	
44	Chard, Thomas P.	55	Retired	
42	Oliver, Charles R.	35	Credit manager	Cambridge
40	Cunningham, Sydney	35	Bookkeeper	Winthrop
24	Kindahl, Frederick	68	Teamster	same
20	Underhill, Edward E.	26	Custom House officer	"
16	Johnson, Matts	58	Rigger	Cambridge
16	Westhaver, David	22	Clerk	Watertown
16	Flink, Martin	28	Machinist	same
14	Rose, William O.	44	Foreman	Cambridge
14	Cunningham, H. E.	55	Clerk	same
10	Felker, G. C.	60	Musician	
10	O'Brien, John J.	39	Policeman	same
10	Weymouth, Guy	38	Lawyer	"

OAK AVENUE.

No.	Name.	Age.	Occupation.	Residence 1914.
7	Loring, Frank E.	48	Salesman	same
11	Vigneau, Leo. B.	39	Manager	"
11	Leonard, Wm. T.	52	Salesman	"
23	Webster, C. W.	40	Farmer	"
23	Brooks, H. W.	76	Real estate	"
39	Davis, Herbert L.	50	Supt.	"
43	Wendall, Charles B.	40	Coal dealer	"
51	Gray, Robert W.	26	Lawyer	
53	Anderson, Albert J.	29	Real estate	
63	Dougherty, Procter L.	38	Manager	
65	Homer, Sidney M.	35	Accountant	
67	Howes, Benjamin L.	68	Retired	
69	Barrett, Wm.	68	Watchman	
75	Anderson, John	63	Clerk	
75	Anderson, Alfred W.	37	Salesman	
75	Anderson, Louis A.	22	Bookkeeper	
75	Dow, Frank R.	28	Accountant	"
97	Rosenberger, Fred B.	33	Com. traveller	Cambridge
92	Dering, H. P. F.	36	Manager	Common st.
62	Norris, Edmund H.	48	Bank clerk	same
60	Lane, Josiah F.	60	Bookkeeper	
32	Giles, John R.	42	Banker	same
28	Gould, Charles H.	60	Granite dealer	"

OAKLEY ROA

No.	Name.	Age.	Occupation.
23	Mullen, Raymond	25	Contractor

OAKLEY ROAD, - Continued.

No.	Name.	Age.	Occupation.	Residence 1914.
23	Mullen, William B.	54	Contractor	same
75	Benton, Everett C.	52	Insurance	"
75	Benton, Charles E.	28	"	"
70	Moltman, Wm. J.	55	Auditor	Arlington
70	Mack, John H.	29	Salesman	Brighton
54	Delano, Frank W.	35	Hatter	same
54	Longridge, Thomas S.	32	Private secretary	"
52	Morash, Fred	33	Builder	"
48	Carrington, Fitzroy	45	Curator	
38	McArdle, James W.	50	Contractor	
20	Dudley, Howland	41	Lawyer	"

OXFORD AVENUE.

3	Boyer, Richard P.	30	Estimator	same
3	Over, Chester H.	27	Bookkeeper	Somerville
3	Mason, Wendell F.	24	Salesman	same
5	Conroy, Michael J.	42	"	"
13	Levin, Zelim	50	Draughtsman	"
15	Dahl, Edward	55	Steamfitter	
17	Swain, Wm. C.	33	Electrical operator	
17	Pollard, Adrian	41	Rubber worker	
17	Reed, Byron W.	32	Lawyer	
23	Gruhn, Adolph A.	23	Butcher	
23	Gruhn, Fred W.	54	"	
23	Patrick, Harrie	26	Clerk	
78	Sjolander, John O.	39	Carpenter	
76	Wolcott, Oliver	28	Printer	
72	Hellen, Oscar	54	Cabinet maker	"
72	Hellen, Rudolph	27	Cabinet maker	same
70	Smith, Thomas J.	44	Brass moulder	"
58	Murphy, James A.	32	Salesman	Penn.
58	Christiansen, Ralph L.	23	Chauffeur	Grove st.
56	Lagerblade, August A.	45	Organ builder	same
56	Remington, Chas. E.	32	Foreman	"
50	Matheson, J. C.	23	Machinist	"
50	Matheson, C. B.	29	Engineer	
50	Baxter, Walter C.	30	Bookkeeper	
50	Gustafson, John F.	31	Chauffeur	
50	Richards, Earle R.	32	Civil engineer	
48	Alger, C. W.	62	Retired	
48	Alger, Harry E.	34	Iron worker	"
48	Baker, Edward A.	41	Teaming	
48	Bowman, Alfred	38	Electrician	Lexington
24	Massey, William T.	30	Salesman	same
24	Meek, Samuel	78	Retired	"
14	Newman, Edward F.	22	Bookkeeper	"
14	Newman, Christopher	58	Shipper	
12	Powers, Richard M.	29	Architect	
10	Mee, Patrick	49	Motorman	

PARK ROAD.

No.	Name.	Age.	Occupation.	Residence 1914.
5	Blair, James	74	Proof reader	same
9	Olson, Chas.	55	Carpenter	"
11	Lewis, Arthur F.	38	Clerk	"
13	Smith, Edward A.	36	Manager	
15	Massey, Harry D.	33	Foreman	
17	Johnson, Chas.	48	Steamfitter	
17	Lehr, Hugo	50	Artist	"
17	Swanson, Manfred	33	Carpenter	Concord ave.
21	Metcalf, Albert S.	34	Electrician	same
23	Landrigan, Patrick J.	36	Salesman	"
23	Mattsson, Victor	34	Painter	Roxbury
27	Frye, Winthrop B.	21	Window dresser	Andover
26	Specht, Alden S.	36	Cheif Engr.	same
26	Lalor, Edmond I.	28	Chauffeur	"
22	Loomer, P. F.	42	Carpenter	"
22	Lindley, F. B.	43	Salesman	Watertown
22	Mehaig, Robert R.	53	Shipper	same
16	Kanaly, Paul J.	21	Clerk	"
16	Kanaly, Morris E.	24	Electrician	"
14	Duncan, Andrew	47	Carpenter	
12	Kidder, Melvin	70	"	
10	Stewart, A. V.	34	Heating engr.	
2	Allen, Alonzo	50	Carpenter	
2	Loomer, Guy	50	"	
45	Bryan, W. James	30	Salesman	Cambridge
45	Fuessel, Geo. G.	35	"	Brookline
47	Prescott, Frank J.	27	Insurance inspector	same
47	Auerbach, Ernest	56	Salesman	Dorchester
57	Marean, Henry E.	36	Salesman	same
281	Lynch, Frank K.	38	Druggist	275 Payson roa
242	Cheney, Nathan C.	40	Mechanical eng.	same
230	Gill, Harold L.	26	Clerk	"
212	Stewart, Arthur M.	61	Real estate & insurance	Cambridge
210	Reed, Albert H.	45	Baker	same
200	Dow, James A.	70	Doctor	"
186	Castle William E.	48	Teacher	"
142	Blaikie, Suther	62	Real estate	
142	Blaikie, Albert	23	Student	"
92	Willison, Elmer C.	50	Salesman	Newton Centre
92	Willison, Howard W.	24	" "	" "
92	Gladwin, C. A.	72	Broker	same
85	Merriam, C. R.	32	Y. M. C. A. secretary	Penn.
84	White, Frank S.	25	Salesman	Watertown
84	White, Herbert M.	34	"	"
72	Wentworth, Miles S.	33	Contractor	same
68	Moore, H. S.	30	Hardware	"

PAYSON ROAD, - Continued.

No.	Name.	Age.	Occupation.	Residence 1914.
58	Schrader, Carl L.	41	Instructor	same
50	Russell, Elmer A.	58	Mfg. confectioner	Cambridge
	Wisdom, Arthur A.	36	Clerk	same
	Andrews, Horatio L.	32	Dentist	Cambridge
	Plunkett, A. J.	37	Manager	Boston

PEQUOSSETTE ROAD.

	Benton, Jay R.	29	Lawyer	same

PINE STREET.

13	Lowrance, John W.	28	Instructor	New Haven
17	Kimball, Clarence	36	Salesman	Cambridge
17	McCuen, Walter C.	32	Manufacturer	same
21	Huse, C. P.	32	Teacher	Missouri
21	Hudson, Harry W.	33	Electrician	Boston
25	Kelly, Thomas A.	55	Salesman	same
25	Curtis, Sydney	34	Secretary	"
31	Hall, Harold T.	34	Surgical goods	6 Marion road
31	Embury, Charles C.	46	Foreman	same
35	Wheeler, Frank E.	62	Piano inspector	"
35	Lord, Frederick T.	50	Manufacturer	"
39	Crocker, Josiah H.	43	Trav. salesman	Cambridge
39	Drawbridge, Robert W.	45	Clergyman	same
41	Howes, Clifton A.	42	Electrical engr.	"
45	Hall, Eben A.	36	Manager	Cambridge
49	Bacon, Fred C.	28	Clerk	"
51	Christman, Geo. Jr.	25	Dentist	17 Falmouth st.
51	Christman, Geo.	52	Foreman	" " "
77	Berry, Harry F.	34	Electrical contractor	Cambridge
77	Morse, Charles F.	40	Manager	Brooklyn, N. Y.
87	McCoy, Hugh A.	46	Tel. supt.	Lowell
87	Leavitt, F. C.	42	Physician	N. Y.
111	Sprague, Willard H.	38	Treasurer	same
115	Robinson, E. J.	49	Builder	"
121	Cameron, Russell	30	Hardware	"
125	Gullifer, Harry	52	Foreman	"
125	Gullifer, Wm. H.	21	Student	
94	Annis, Everett F.	43	Decorator	Cambridge
90	Lowry, Kieran J.	35	Supt. B. A. A. Boston	"
90	Raddin, Thomas	34	Electrical engr.	17 Bartlett road.
64	Belcher, Geo. A.	43	Salesman	same
62	Grotjohn, Philip F.	40	Machinist	"
50	Van Doren, J. Edward	38	Insurance	Dorchester
44	Olson, Carl	39	Sculptor	same
38	Baxter, Wm. F.	35	Teller	Arlington
28	Wood, James F.	34	Salesman	same

PINE STREET, - Continued.

28	Slayter, Henry S.	48	Manufacturer	Cambridge
22	Thulin, Walfred	38	Wood carver	same
20	Hart, John P.	38	Compositor	"
14	McKee, Fred W.	32	Salesman	"
14	McCuen, Fred J.	40	...	"

SCHOOL STREET.

375	Wood, Isaac P.	82	Retired	same
375	Hittinger, Charles F.	60	Market gardener	"
431	Vethas, Parvel	22	Farm hand	Unknown
431	Norton, Michael F.	35	Foreman	same
493	Keefe, Patrick	56	Farm hand	"
468	Richardson, James M.	30	Market gardener	"

SPRINGFIELD STREET.

11	Tapley, Albert A.	56	Salesman	same
17	Greene, Walter	32	"	"
19	Hanf, Adolf	43	Machinist	"
21	McReavy, H. L.	38	Commission merchant	"
23	Baxter, Thompson S.	35	Electrician	
28	Morse, Edward	26	Chauffeur	..
28	Morse, James E. Jr.	22	"	"
28	Morse, James E.	48	Painter	"
12	Chase, Harry S.	31	Printer	"
6	Eldridge, Arthur L.	26	Salesman	Salem
6	Butler, Walter L.	30	Janitor	same
6	Moffat, Albert S.	28	Electrical Engr.	"
6	Rockwell, Wallace L.	26		Boston

7	Gray, Norman A.	25	Paymaster	Winthrop
7	Andrews, S. M.	41	Merchant	Allston
6	Seaverance, Leon M.	24	Manager	Arlington
	Cabot, Walter K.	30	Mechanical engr.	Cambridge
	Rowley, Leonard W.	27	Salesman	Douglass
	Trenholm, C. E.		Real estate & insurance	Cambridge
	Huddy, Frederick L.	35	Diamond setter	Boston

TRAPELO R

100	Nickerson, Mortimer	40	Asst. manager	Chelsea
98	Robinson, Roy L.	30	Grocer	same
96	Blennerhassett, Arthur	49	Sexton	"

TRAPELO ROAD, - Continued.

No.	Name.	Age.	Occupation.	Residence 1914
94	Kelley, James W.	42	Customs examiner	same
92	Simpson, Hiram L.	62	Confectionery	"
90	Norton, Harry E.	24	Salesman	Penn.
90	Norton, William M.	31	"	Boston
88	Brock, O. H.	60	Hardware	Cambridge
86	Conklin, Fred B.	45	Salesman	same
72	Hawthorne, Robert	33	Groom	Brookline

UNITY AVENUE.

No.	Name.	Age.	Occupation.	Residence 1914
33	Anderson, Olof N.	53	Foreman	44 Dartmouth st.
41	Reader, George	26	Carpenter	Cambridge
41	Meek, Spratt M.	45	Hardware	same
57	Brown, Henry A.	52	Machinist	"
61	Hanley, Chas. C.	48	Pressman	"
78	Calnan, James S.	49	Postal clerk	"
76	Waldo, William R.	28	Estimator	25 Falmouth st.

WASHINGTON STREET.

No.	Name.	Age.	Occupation.	Residence 1914
51	Binkly, Jay N.	48	Salesman	same
101	Anthony, John	35	Farmer	Chalmont
161	Jackson, Frank	65	Retired	same
161	Jackson, Phillip S.	22	Watchmaker	"
·161	Chenery, Chas. H.	48	Farmer	"
215	Shaw, Edward H.	30	Market gardener	"
245	Hodgdon, Frank M.	31	Salesman	Trapelo road
275	Shaw, Fred H.	26	Farmer	same

W STREET.

No.	Name.	Age.	Occupation.	Residence 1914
17	Bradbury, Henry	38	Salesman	Arlington
27	Harris, Geo. A.	44	Clerk	same
31	Van Wyck, Clarence B.	43	Secretary	"
33	Stonemetz, John C.	35	Broker	"
33	Reynolds, Joseph G. Jr.	28	Designer	
39	Merrow, Chas. F.	35	Manager	
45	Walker, Wm. H.	34	Auditor	
45	Johnston, Andrew N.	62	Foreman	
52	Odde, John A. L.	38	Lawyer	
32	Long, Albert B.	63	Retired	"
	Drew, Frederick J.	58	Insurance	Boston

WORCESTER STREET.

No.	Name.	Age.	Occupation.	Residence 1914
8	Drake, Everett W.	32	Bookkeeper	same

WORCESTER STREET, - Continued.

No.	Name.	Age.	Occupation.	Residence 1914.
6	Malmstrom, Nils	25	Dentist	same
6	Malmstrom, Vitalis	45	Piano finisher	"
6	Preble, Leverett L.	36	Instructor	"
4	Park, O. J.	50	Builder	Stoneham
2	Howard, John	56	Foreman	same
2	Buck, Charles W.	81	Retired	"

NOTE.--The word "same" refers to the street of last year's residence, the number not alwa being the same.

ALPHABETICAL LIST OF POLLS.

TOWN OF BELMONT, 1915.

NAME.	NO.	STREET.	NAME.	NO	STREET.
Abbott, E. Stanley	592	Pleasant st.	Arenstrop, Henry F.	70	Somerset st.
Abbott, Frank A.	51	Maple st.	Argy, John	124	Beech st.
Adams, Earl	64	Agassiz av.	Armitage, John S.		Pleasant st.
Adams, Franklin W.	48	Agassiz av.	Armstrong, George P.	1	Clover st.
Adams, William L.	5	Sunnyside pl.	Arno, Giovanni	65	Walnut st.
Addessa, Tony	40	Maple st.	Arno, Joseph	65	Walnut st.
Ahearn, John		Pleasant st.	Arno, Joseph	26	Thomas st.
Aiken, William	39	Agassiz av.	Arno, Nino	65	Walnut st.
Alberto, Carnio	38	Grant av.	Arno, Paul	11	Walnut st.
Alcock, Samuel	20	Cutter st.	Arno, Tony	26	Thomas st.
Alexander, Alec	7	Ash st.	Arnold, Charles A.	41	Lexington st.
Alger, C. W.	48	Oxford av.	Arnoldson, Frank	11	Marion rd.
Alger, Ernest E.	61	Waverley st.	Arrington, Arthur W.	175	Belmont st.
Alger, Frank W.	61	Waverley st.	Atkins, Edwin F.	580	Concord av.
Alger, Harry E.	48	Oxford av.	Atkins, Edwin F. Jr.	580	Concord av.
Alger, James H.	61	Waverley st.	Atkinson, William T.	13	Maple st.
Ali, Joseph	7	B st.	Atwell, Andrew Y.	46	Lexington st.
Allen, Alonzo	2	Park rd.	Auerbach, Ernest	47	Payson rd.
Allen, Charles A.	17	Cutter st.	Augustine, Frank	7	B st.
Allyn, S. Bradford	113	Leonard st.	Austin, George	83	School st.
Almgren, Axel	23	Marion rd.	Austin, Newell B.	68	Waverley st.
Almgren, George W.	34	Falmouth st.	Avery, Niram	138	Waverley st.
Alput, Julius S.	45	Dartmouth st.	Ayer, Lucius	15	Moraine st.
Alt, James	91	Beech st.	Bacon, Fred C.	49	Pine st.
Amastas, Panos	140	White st.	Bacon, George H.	64	Leonard st.
Amastas, Peter	140	White st.	Bacon, Henry A.	64	Leonard st.
Amastas, Tony		David rd.	Baer, Anton	13	Cambridge st.
Anderson, Albert J.	53	Oak av.	Baer, Otto	13	Cambridge st.
Anderson, Alfred W.	75	Oak av.	Bailey, Alfred	67	Agassiz av.
Anderson, Axel D.	416	Trapelo rd.	Bailey, Howard C.	48	Falmouth st.
Anderson, Gustaf	15	Marion rd.	Baker, Alden, F.	18	Frederick st.
Anderson, H. Samuel	35	Concord av.	Baker, Arthur	off	Pleasant st.
Anderson, James H.	17	Bartlett rd.	Baker, Cassius H.	229	Belmont st.
Anderson, John	75	Oak av.	Baker, Edward A.	48	Oxford av.
Anderson, John	4	Exeter st.	Baker, Taylor	20	Ericsson st.
Anderson, Lars A.	140	Beech st.	Balch, George L.		Pleasant st.
Anderson, Louis A.	75	Oak av.	Baldwin, Harry H.	568	Pleasant st.
Anderson, Olof N.	33	Unity av.	Baldwin, Harry Jr.	568	Pleasant st.
Andrelo, John	17	Grant av.	Baldwin, Walter F.	31	Marion rd.
Andrews, Arthur W.	43	Burnham st.	Balough, Bertram	164	Beech st.
Andrews, Eben F.	11	Lexington st.	Banfil, Jerrold W.	19	Marion rd.
Andrews, Edward F.	43	Burnham st.	Banks, Amos L.	214	White st.
Andrews, Everett E.	52	Burnham st.	Barker, Albert H.	10	Waverley st.
Andrews, Frank	50	Lexington st.	Barnes, George H.	27	Harriet av.
Andrews, Harry A.	11	Moraine st.	Barnes, Harry T.	48	Waverley st.
Andrews, Horatio L.		Payson rd.	Barnes, Israel M.	2	Thayer st.
Andrews, Melvin C.	81	Dartmouth st.	Barnes, Wales G.	29	Harriet av.
Andrews, Newell D.	37	Burnham st.	Barney, Charles	19	Hawthorn st.
Andrews, S. M.	7	Townsend rd.	Barrett, Fred O.	308	Waverley st.
Angell, Ernest F.	off	White st.	Barrett, Jos. F.	83	Beech st.
Angell, James G.	22	Marion rd.	Barrett, William	69	Oak av.
Angelo, Frank	200	Beech st.	Barrows, Alvin S.	20	Moraine st.
Angelo, Michael	15	Walnut st.	Barrows, James A.	20	Moraine st.
Annis, Everett F.	94	Pine st.	Barry, Michael J.	46	Grove st.
Annis, Frank		Pleasant st.	Bartlett, George O.	437	Trapelo rd.
Anthony, John	101	Washington st.	Bartsch, Herman H.	38	Moraine st.
Annuziata, Luigi	52	Grant av.	Barton, Charles A.		Howells rd.
Ardrie, C. Cornish		Pleasant st.	Bates, Fred O.		Hillside ter.
Arena, Harry	67	Concord av.	Bathrick, John J.	29	Oak st.
Arena, Joseph	67	Concord av.	Batiste, Saveuo	23	Underwood st.

ALPHABETICAL LIST OF POLLS.—Con.

NAME.	NO.	STREET.	NAME.	NO.	STREET.
Baxter, Frank W.	55	Dartmouth st.	Blake, Harry E.	91	Beech st.
Baxter, Herbert L.	75	Marlboro st.	Blanchard, Michael P.	10	Moraine st.
Baxter, James J.	116	Common st.	Blanchard, Munroe A.	off	Thomas st.
Baxter, Thompson S.	23	Springfield st.	Blennerhassett, Arthur	96	Trapelo rd.
Baxter, Walter C.	50	Oxford av.	Bliss, Franklin H.	73	Marlboro st.
Baxter, William F.	38	Pine st.	Blodgett, George E.	27	Cutter st.
Beals, George A.	51	Moraine st.	Blomquist, Olof	56	Dartmouth s
Beals, William	47	Maple st.	Blood, Wallace S.	67	Berwick st.
Beals, William A.	51	Moraine st.	Blurn, W. J.		Pleasant st.
Bear, John R.	15	Marlboro st.	Boissonade, Charles J.	9	Hull st.
Beardsley, Crowell E.	139	Belmont st.	Boissoneau, Eugene	109	Concord av.
Beaton, Herbert L.	8	Oak st.	Bollinger, J. Guy		Pleasant st.
Beaton, Peter A.	8	Oak st.	Bollinger, T. Frank		Pleasant st.
Beatson, Jesse W.	55	Dartmouth st.	Bonan, Peter	7	B st.
Beck, Carl O.	17	Concord av.	Bonney, Robert D.	5	Concord av.
Becker, William C.	163	Beech st.	Booth, Sydney S.	325	Trapelo rd.
Beckman, William C.		Belmont st.	Boucher, Jos. L.	24	Trowbridge
Bedford, Alfred E.	10	Creeley rd.	Bourden, John		Belmont st.
Beebe, Manley C.	223	White st.	Bourden, Samuel	54	Alma av.
Beebe, Max N.	223	White st.	Bourneuf, Leander F.	2	Cherry st.
Beecher, William J.	11	Maple st.	Bourneuf, William	2	Cherry st.
Beede, E. Jefts	123	School st.	Bowler, Herbert W.	17	Holt st.
Beekman, James G.	138	Beech st.	Bowler, William	12	Chenery ter.
Beeler, Enoch F.	141	Sycamore st.	Bowman, Alfred	48	Oxford av.
Beeler, Fred	16	Thayer rd.	Bowman, William O.	9	Agassiz av.
Beeler, William E.	16	Thayer rd.	Boyer, Rich P.	3	Oxford av.
Beelte, Leslie V.		Lawndale st.	Boyd, James V.	346	Trapelo rd.
Beelte, W. F.		Lawndale st.	Boynton, Geo. H.		Kilburn st.
Belcher, George A.	64	Pine st.	Brabazon, Ed. R.		Pleasant st.
Bella, John	15	Grant av.	Bradbury, Henry	17	Willow st.
Bellantoni, John	38	Leonard st.	Bradbury, John P.	120	White st.
Bellevue, Edward	2	Cherry st.	Bradett, Baptiste	109	Concord av.
Bennett, Edmund	21	Underwood st.	Bradley, James J.	62	Marlboro st
Bennett, Godfrey	21	Underwood st.	Brant, Arthur	83	Beech st.
Bennett, James J.	87	School st.	Brant, Isaac	83	Beech st.
Bennett, John K.	33	Marion st.	Brassil, John E.	64	David rd.
Benoit, Jesse	61	Waverley st.	Brassil, Thomas J.	57	Berwick st.
Benson, Carl	69	Marlboro st.	Brennan, James E.	37	Grove st.
Benson, Gustaf	17	Concord av.	Brennan, Patrick	371	Concord av
Bent, Guy	7	Moraine st.	Bresnan, Cornelius F.	44	Brighton st
Bent, Maurice A.	33	Marlboro st.	Bresnan, Cornelius J.	44	Brighton st
Benton, Charles E.	75	Oakley rd.	Bridgham, Percy A.	41	Waverley s
Benton, Everett C.	75	Oakley rd.	Briggs, Benjamin F.	232	White st.
Benton, Jay R.		Pequossette rd	Briggs, Clarence V.	85	Walnut st.
Berenson, Louis	806	Pleasant st.	Briggs, Frank B.	85	Walnut st.
Berger, Kenneth	12	Falmouth st.	Briggs, James H.	85	Walnut st.
Berry, Harry F.	77	Pine st.	Brock, Ralph L.		Stone rd.
Beverly, C. W.	11	Cutter st.	Brock, O. H.	88	Trapelo rd.
Bickford, Edwin D.	422	Trapelo rd.	Broderick, John F.		Waverley s
Bickmore, George		Pleasant st.	Brodrick, Royal T.	67	Orchard st.
Binkly, Jay N.	51	Washington st	Brooke, Percy A.		Pleasant st.
Birch, Albert	56	Fairmont st.	Brooks, Geo. F. T.	31	Falmouth s
Birch, Clifford W.	56	Fairmont st.	Brooks, H. W.	23	Oak av.
Birch, Harold W.	56	Fairmont st.	Bromley, Samuel J.	24	Wilson av.
Bird, Frank J.	416	Trapelo rd.	Brosnahan, Thomas P.	26	Cross st.
Bisnaro, George A.	off	White st.	Brown, Bertram L.	17	Marion rd.
Blaikie, Albert	142	Payson rd.	Brown, Chester P.	121	Beech st.
Blaikie, Suther	142	Payson rd.	Brown, Edward	206	Waverley s
Blair, James	5	Park rd.	Brown, Edward, Jr.	562	Trapelo rd.
Blair, James A.	215	Belmont st.	Brown, Edward A.		Concord av
Blaisdell, Warren H.	20	Harriet av.	Brown, E. Horace	24	Church st.

Alphabetical List of Polls.—*Con.*

NAME.	NO.	STREET.	NAME.	NO.	STREET.
Brown, Frank E.	34	Ridge rd.	Campbell, Walter	73	Grove st.
Brown, Frank W.	9	Chenery ter.	Cannon, Willard S.	74	Goden st.
Brown, Harold I.	95	Clifton st.	Cannon, Winthrop D.	74	Goden st.
Brown, Henry A.	57	Unity av.	Carey, Harry	38	Grove st.
Brown, James	45	Common st.	Carey, Thomas J.	11	Sunnyside pl.
Brown, James J.	75	Lexington st.	Carlo, Joseph	50	Chandler st.
Brown, John A.	593	Pleasant st.	Carlo, Peter	52	Grant av.
Brown, John H.	440	Common st.	Carlson, Emil	7	Concord av.
Brown, John O.	20	Wilson av.	Carlson, Robert	64	Dartmouth st.
Brown, Stephen S.		Pleasant st.	Carlton, Chas. E.	25	Francis st.
Brown, Thomas R.	4	Marion rd.	Carmichael, Charles		Pleasant st.
Brown, William S.	593	Pleasant st.	Carney, James F.	2	Thomas st.
Brown, Winthrop	45	Common st.	Carney, John J.	281	Waverley st.
Brown, Winthrop Jr.	45	Common st.	Carney, William	140	Common st.
Bruno, Rocco	57	Baker st.	Carr, O. F.	84	Lexington st.
Bruno, Salvator	34	Trowbridge st.	Carr, Paul J.		Pleasant st.
Bryan, Fred	75	Lexington st.	Carrington, Fitzroy,	48	Oakley rd.
Bryan, W. James	45	Payson rd.	Carroll, Leo	10	Moraine st.
Bryant, Melvin H.	22	Thayer rd.	Carroll, Thomas	50	White st.
Bucci, Donato	87	Hull st.	Carroll, William H.	50	White st.
Buck, Charles W.	2	Worcester st.	Carson, James	455	Common st.
Buckley, Daniel	20	Cross st.	Carson, James S.	455	Common st.
Buckley, Daniel	22	Davis rd.	Carson, Robert A.	67	Agassiz av.
Buckley, John	22	Davis rd.	Carter, C. H.	234	White st.
Buckley, Prescott	22	Davis rd.	Carter, Edward A.	33	Moraine st.
Bugney, Walter K.	44	Grove st.	Cary, George H.	106	Sycamore st.
Bump, Albert H.	184	Concord av.	Cary, Ralph H.	104	Sycamore st.
Bump, Henry M.	184	Concord av.	Cashman, Patrick	710	Pleasant st.
Bunker, John P.	55	Maple st.	Cassidy, James	76	Cross st.
Buonfiglio, Tony	40	Walnut st.	Castino, Pedro		A st.
Burdakin, Arthur L.	319	Mill st.	Castle, William E.	186	Payson rd.
Burdakin, Gilbert	319	Mill st.	Castner, Eldorus A.	612	Trapelo rd.
Burke, Daniel	14	Ash st.	Cate, Eleazar	11	Oak st.
Burke, Michael J.	120	Lexington st.	Catton, W. R.	8	Marion rd.
Burke, William H.		Baker st.	Caulfield, George	69	Marlboro st.
Burleigh, Charles	20	Chandler st.	Chaffee, E. Leon	82	Goden st.
Burleigh, Willard G.	20	Chandler st.	Chaffee, Emory F.		Cedar rd.
Burnick, Patrick	24	Cross st.	Chamian, C. H.	7	Ash st.
Burns, Edward A.	34	Maple st.	Chandler, F. Alex.	90	Lexington st.
Burns, Edward F. P.	51	Berwick st.	Chandler, Oscar M.	128	School st.
Burns, John A.	480	Concord av.	Channal, William	36	Maple st.
Burrage, Paul	235	Belmont st.	Chant, Frank D.	40	Concord av.
Burrell, Charles A.	408	Trapelo rd.	Chapman, Loring T.	17	Francis st.
Burrows, Gordon	228	Waverley st.	Chard, Thomas P.	44	Marlboro st.
Busby, Fred H.	5	Vincent av.	Chase, Chas.		Kilburn rd.
Busby, Warren	35	Marion rd.	Chase, Harry S.	12	Springfield st.
Bushway, James H.	69	Berwick st.	Chausey, Maxime E.	5	Exeter st.
Butchard, David	off	Thomas st.	Chenery, Chas. E.	52	Washington st
Butchard, David	off	Thomas st.	Chenery, Chas. K.	161	Washington st
Butler, Walter L.	6	Springfield st.	Chenery, David	325	Common st.
Cabot, Walter K.		Townsend rd.	Chenery, Franklin W.	325	Common st.
Cahill, Thomas P.	96	Sycamore st.	Chenery, George W.	52	Washington st
Cain, George H.	12	Goden st.	Cheney, Nathan C.	242	Payson rd.
Callabro, Joseph	52	Thomas st.	Cherry, Arthur B.	179	Belmont st.
Callaban, Henry F.	148	Beech st.	Cherry, Charles W.		David rd.
Callahan, Wm. A.	66	Leonard st.	Cherry, Leslie R.	22	Davis rd.
Calnan, James S.	78	Unity av.	Cherry, Thomas H.		David rd.
Camack, David	422	Trapelo rd.	Cherry, Williard E.	208	White st.
Camack, William A.	422	Trapelo rd.	Cheshire, George	244	Brighton st.
Cameron, Russell	121	Pine st.	Chick, Harry W.	328	Pleasant st.
Campbell, Henry		Heustis rd.	Chisholm, Roderick A. J.		Pleasant st.

ALPHABETICAL LIST OF POLLS.—*Con.*.

NAME.	NO.	STREET.	NAME.	NO.	STREET.
Chisholm, William D.		Pleasant st.	Cook, Chas. W.	7	Ericsson st.
Chism, John	123	Beech st.	Cook, Joseph E.	7	Ericsson st.
Christiansen, Ralph L.	58	Oxford av.	Cook, Joseph E. Jr.	7	Ericsson st.
Christiansen, Norman	87	Grove st.	Cooksley, Alfred	22	Whitcomb st.
Christie, William H.	115	Lexington st.	Cooksley, Daniel	22	Whitcomb st.
Christman, Geo.	51	Pine st.	Coole, Gerald W.		Pleasant st.
Christman, Geo. Jr.	51	Pine st.	Coombs, Martin A.	25	Falmouth st.
Churchill, Gilman	15	Lawndale st.	Cooper, A. H.	215	Belmont st.
Clancy, Norman N.	11	Agassiz st.	Cooper, Frederick J.	9	Ericsson st.
Clark, Herbert A.	519	Pleasant st.	Cooper, Sidney F.	9	Ericsson st.
Clark, J. Frank	96	Sycamore st.	Corbett, Alex. E.	37	Waverley st.
Clark John		Concord av.	Corbett, Charles W.		Pearl st.
Clark, Dr. Leonard B.	36	Sycamore st.	Corcoran, John F.	87	Fairview av.
Clark, Lyman O.	58	Harriet av.	Corcoran, Michael J.	87	Fairview av.
Clark, Walter B.	58	Harriet av.	Corey, Fred A.	181	Lexington st
Clarke, William J.	136	Sycamore st.	Cormey, Alexander	251	Waverley st.
Claus, Robert C.	22	Burnham st.	Cormey, Frederick J.	251	Waverley st.
Clausen, Holger W.	62	Marlboro st.	Cosgrove, James W.	65	Grove st.
Clausen, Peter W.	62	Marlboro st.	Costello, Michael	26	Wilson av.
Cleland, Fred E.	467	Pleasant st.	Costine, James	340	Lake st.
Cleland, Frank	200	Waverley st.	Costine, Patrick	62	Thomas st.
Clement, William	238	White st.	Cotter, Michael	306	Washington
Clisby, John P.	41	Waverley st.	Cough, Edward J.	155	Beech st.
Clunan, Patrick J.	12	Woodland st.	Courtney, Daniel J.	410	Trapelo rd.
Cobb, Howard P.	58	Dartmouth st.	Courtney, William J.	87	Grove st.
Cochran, Myron J.		Trapelo rd.	Cox, Michael H.	4	Goden st.
Cochrane, Alex. Y.	544	Trapelo rd.	Cox, William T.	54	Burnham st.
Cody, Hugh	68	Agassiz av.	Craig, Joseph	19	Davis rd.
Coe, John W.	9	Falmouth st.	Craven, William	17	Baker st.
Coe, Rev. Reginald H.		Prospect st.	Crawford, Alex.	592	Trapelo rd.
Coen, Dennis M.	9	Hull st.	Crawford, Arthur A.	30	Falmouth st.
Coen, Michael	107	Beech st.	Creeley, Thomas L.	375	Common st.
Cogan, William H.	16	Chandler st.	Crine, William	176	Waverley st.
Cohen, Michael	59	Thomas st.	Crispo, Fred		Pleasant st.
Cokinos, George	140	White st.	Crocker, Chas.		Prospect st.
Cokinos, Nicholas J.	140	White st.	Crocker, George R.	410	Trapelo rd.
Colburn, Chas. E.	44	Clark st.	Crocker, Josiah H.	39	Pine st.
Colburn, Chas. L.	51	Harriet av.	Crocker, Robert	174	Lexington st
Cole, James T.	15	Clover st.	Crocker, Philander R.	23	Myrtle st.
Coleman, Daniel	68	Agassiz av.	Cronin, John	180	Waverley st.
Coleman, J. E.	36	Church st.	Cronin, William P.		School st.
Colliers, Frank L.	26	Orchard st.	Crook, Robert	171	Beech st.
Collins, Nelson A.	25	Cutter st.	Crowell, Clarence O.	50	Lexington s
Collins, Patrick	321	Concord av.	Crowell, William F.	80	Cushing av.
Collins, Thomas	43	Thomas st.	Crowley, John J.	21	Underwood s
Collinson, Claude M. B.	212	Lexington st.	Crowley, Simon	76	Cross st.
Comeau, Frank		Alexander av.	Cucinotta, Giovanni	65	Walnut st.
Comeau, Louis	10	Cherry st.	Cuffe, James A.	42	Falmouth st
Conant, Chas. B.	51	Berwick st.	Culhane, Daniel	43	Marion rd.
Condon, Timothy	253	Waverley st.	Cullici, Joseph	11	Walnut st.
Conklin, Fred B.		Trapelo rd.	Cullici, Nino	11	Walnut st.
Conlon, Joseph L.	105	Beech st.	Cullici, Paul	11	Walnut st.
Connell, James W.		Walnut st.	Cummings, Chas. F.	15	Marlboro st.
Connelly, Dennis F.	112	Waverley st.	Cummings, Chas. H.	114	Belmont st.
Connor, William N.	32	Ridge rd.	Cummings, John	194	Waverley st.
Connors, John	156	Waverley st.	Cummings, John J.	10	Holt st.
Conrey, Karl S.	339	Trapelo rd.	Cummings, Richard J. J.	113	Belmont st.
Conroy, Michael J.	5	Oxford av.	Cunningham, Dr. E. A.	175	Belmont st.
Constanino, Salvator	7	B st.	Cunningham, Michael E.	548	Trapelo rd.
Convinen, Frank	40	Baker st.	Cunningham, H. E.	14	Marlboro st.
Cook, Chas. S.	6	Moraine st.	Cunningham, Sydney	40	Marlboro st.

ALPHABETICAL LIST OF POLLS.—*Con.*

NAME.	NO.	STREET.	NAME.	NO.	STREET.
Cupid, Alex.	93	Beech st.	Dillon, Edwin, S.	19	Lawndale st.
Cupid, Alex. G.		Pleasant st.	Dillon, Stephen N.	19	Lawndale st.
Curley, Mitchell	248	Mill st.	Dimick, Joseph H.	6	Ericsson st.
Curley, Owen S.	63	Hull st.	Dixon, Geo.	152	Brighton st.
Curry, Joseph A.	31	Francis st.	Dodge, Frank W.	36	Thayer rd.
Curtin, William W.	15	Woodland st.	Dodge, Frederic	59	Clark st.
Curtis, Sydney	25	Pine st.	Dodge, George H.	60	Harriet av.
Cushing, Edward O.	8	Thayer st.	Doherty, John		Pleasant st.
Cushman, George M.	330	Pleasant st.	Dolan, Rev. Gerald L.	116	Common st.
Cutter, George H.		Hillside ter.	Dole, Albion, B.	20	Cambridge st.
Cutler, William J.	605	Pleasant st.	Donahue, John		Goden st.
Cutler, Wolcott	605	Pleasant st.	Donahue, Patrick	14	Midland st.
Dacey, James	15	Leonard st.	Donahue, Robert	14	Midland st.
Dadeski, Philip	42	Grant av.	Donahue, Thomas	14	Midland st.
Daghlian, Harontune		Pleasant st.	Donahue, William	14	Midland st.
Dahl, Edward	15	Oxford av.	Donle, Earl R.		Benjamin rd.
Dakin, George H.	44	Dartmouth st.	Donovan, Dennis	176	Waverley st.
Daley, John	17	Maple ter.	Donovan, Timothy	20	Cross st.
Daley, Patrick	rear 343	Pleasant st.	Dorney, John T.	87	Grove st.
Daley, P. J.	17	Maple ter.	Dougherty Proctor L.	63	Oak av.
Dally, John	57	Grant av.	Douglas, Arthur L.	47	Thomas st.
Daly, John	214	Waverley st.	Douglass, William H.	628	Trapelo rd.
Daly, John	54	Marlboro st.	Douthart, R. S.	177	Belmont st.
Daly, John F.	217	White st.	Dow, Frank R.	75	Oak av.
Daly, M. J.	16	Church st.	Dow, James A.	200	Payson rd.
Daly, Thomas A.	606	Trapelo rd.	Dow, Oscar W.	70	Waverley st.
Dana, Edward		Bright rd.	Dowd, William	480	Concord av.
Danforth, William J.	49	Marlboro st.	Doyle, Edmund	29	Hawthorn st.
Dasma, Antro	9	B st.	Doyle, Frederick L.	57	Grove st.
Davis, Allan M.	16	Chandler st.	Drake, Everett W.	8	Worcester st.
Davis, Daniel L.	86	Clifton st.	Drawbridge, Robert W.	39	Pine st.
Davis, Geo. W.	86	Clifton st.	Drayton, Frank O.	62	Sycamore st.
Davis, Harry C.	28	Bartlett rd.	Dresser, George	140	Beech st.
Davis, Herbert E.	86	Clifton st.	Drew, Ernest L.		Linden av.
Davis, Herbert L.	39	Oak av.	Drew, Frederick J.		Willow st.
Davis, Ralph	55	Waverley st.	Driscoll, Henry	63	Underwood st.
Davison, F. A.	12	Davis rd.	Driscoll, Thomas	63	Underwood st.
Deehan, Frank E.	7	Davis rd.	Drisken, Roger	70	Somerset st.
Delagatto, James	9	Grant av.	Drolette, Joseph	105	Concord av.
Delano, Frank W.	54	Oakley rd.	Dudley, Howland	20	Oakley rd.
Delany, Edmund H.	56	Berwick st.	Dudley, Warren P.	14	Oak st.
Delmastro, Dominick	17	Underwood st.	Duffley, James F.	99	Beech st.
DeMond, Frank S.	46	Lexington st.	Dugan, Charles F.	15	Woodland st.
DeMond, Geo. A.	46	Lexington st.	Dugan, Peter	15	Woodland st.
Dennett, L. Guy	19	Burnham st.	Dugan, Peter A.	15	Woodland st.
Depasquali, Tony	38	Leonard st.	Dunbar, Harold C.	5	Spinney ter.
Dering, H. P. F.	92	Oak av.	Duncan, Andrew	14	Park rd.
Descoteaux, George N.		Benjamin rd.	Duncan, Oscar W.	24	Davis rd.
Desillve, Joseph	140	White st.	Dunn, Winfield T.	426	Trapelo rd.
Desmond, Jer.	13	Grant av.	Dunning, George H.	14	Orchard st.
Desmond, Patrick	13	Grant av.	Dunnell, Harry R.	56	Berwick st.
Desmond, William	16	Moraine st.	Dunnell, James A.	56	Berwick st.
De Stefano, Franseco	45	Trowbridge st.	Dunsford, Isaac	385	Concord av.
Devany, Dr. Patrick A.	62	White st.	Duplessis, Nelson K.	225	Belmont st.
De Vito, A. Ralph	20	Trowbridge st.	Dutcher, C. F.	16	Church st.
Dewey, Percy		Hillcrest rd.	Dutra, Joseph J.	30	Hawthorn st.
Dickerson, John	117	Beech st.	Egan, John J.	43	Concord av.
Dickinson, Eben C.	7	Marion rd.	Earle, Arthur J.	48	Bartlett av.
Dill, Geo. N.	85	Concord av.	Eaton, Chas. A.		Pleasant st.
Dill, Joseph H.	85	Concord av.	Edgar, John	43	Lexington st.
Dillon, Albert W.	10	Frederick st.	Edmonstone, William M.	142	Waverley st.

ALPHABETICAL LIST OF POLLS.—*Con.*

NAME.	NO.	STREET.	NAME.	NO.	STREET.
Edwards, John	28	Burnham st.	Fisher, Hugh	27	Chandler st.
Egan, Patrick J.	23	Thomas st.	Fisher, James	45	Chandler st.
Eglin, Ernest	45	Marlboro st.	Fisher, James H.	45	Chandler st.
Eigenfeldt, John	439	Pleasant st.	Fisher, John	41	Lexington st
Eisnor, Fred A.	11	Lexington st.	Fisher, John R.	155	Beech st.
Elder, Chas.	426	Trapelo rd.	Fitch, Wilbur R.	56	Falmouth st.
Elder, Robert	66	Mill st.	Fitz. Norman E.	416	Trapelo rd.
Eldridge, Arthur L.	6	Springfield st.	Fitzgerald, Edward G.	33	Wilson av.
Elertson, Emil	40	Grove st.	Fitzgerald, John	25	Chandler st.
Elias, Joseph	168	Waverley st.	Fitzpatrick, Frank A.	34	Centre av.
Elliott, James E.	29	Myrtle st.	Flanders, Charles E.	11	Cutter st.
Ellis, J. Lucius	147	Lexington st.	Fleck, Matthew	1034	Pleasant st.
Ellis, Leopold	81	Lexington st.	Fleming, David J.	9	Agassiz av.
Ellison, Frank D.	44	Clark st.	Fleming, John	off	Concord av.
Ellison, William H.	410	Common st.	Fleming, Richard	76	Cross st.
Ellsworth, Henry E.	25	Falmouth st.	Fleming, William H.	9	Agassiz av.
Elson, Alfred W.	527	Concord av.	Fletcher, Arthur	439	Pleasant st.
Embury, Charles C.	31	Pine st.	Fletcher, Elmer A.	184	Washington s
Emerson, Chas.	57	Marlboro st.	Fletcher, Geo. V.	483	Pleasant st.
Emerson, George C.	67	Berwick st.	Fletcher, H. L.	16	Marion rd.
Emery, James W.	299	Waverley st.	Fletcher, J. Henry	439	Pleasant st.
Emily, Harold	90	Somerset st.	Fletcher, Richmond K.	42	Falmouth st.
Engstrom, Herman A.	171	Beech st.	Flett, George C.	596	Trapelo rd.
Enos, George		Pleasant st.	Flett, J. Watson	596	Trapelo rd.
Epps, Frederick H.	23	Waverley st.	Flett, W. Leonard	8	Cherry st.
Erickson, Arvid	61	Dartmouth st.	Flewelling, Fred	51	White st.
Erickson, John	61	Dartmouth st.	Flink, Martin	16	Marlboro st.
Erickson, John C.	61	Dartmouth st.	Flint, Lester E.	94	Stone rd.
Ericson, Oscar	385	Concord av.	Flynn, Andrew F.	128	Sycamore st.
Erstby, Gothard	37	Marlboro st.	Flynn, John F.	128	Sycamore st.
Esters, Clarence E.	32	Maple st.	Fogarty, George F.	32	Maple st.
Ewell, Thomas B.	25	Falmouth st.	Fogerty, James L.	99	Beech st.
Fadden, James		Pleasant st.	Fogg, Alton T.	65	Grove st.
Fagan, James O.	17	Cutter st.	Follett, Leslie C.	67	Berwick st.
Fagerstrowm, John		Pleasant st.	Fonte, Salvatore	17	Grant av.
Fairbanks, James	29	Francis st.	Foote, Henry S.	546	Trapelo rd.
Faircloth, Wm. F.	22	Trowbridge st.	Forand, Delphis C.	14	Davis rd.
Fallon, Mat.	194	Waverley st.	Ford, Thomas	14	Cottage st.
Fanning, John F.	51	Marion rd.	Ford, Walter F.	99	Beech st.
Farmer, Fred		Pleasant st.	Foster, David H.	7	Vincent av.
Farmer, Geo. T.	6	Ericsson st.	Foster, Lewis W.	229	Belmont st.
Farmer, John	541	Trapelo rd.	Fowler, C. R.	10	Marion rd.
Farnham, Edwin E.	560	Pleasant st.	Frain, Thomas P.		Pleasant st.
Farrell, Albert L.	347	Trapelo rd.	Franscali, Guy	24	Trowbridge
Farrington, Daniel	144	Sycamore st.	Frehrickson, Fritz W.	51	Berwick st.
Farwell, Edward C.	55	Berwick st.	Freeman, Carl	218	Lake st.
Feeney, Joseph P.	125	Belmont st.	Freeman, William H.	25	Wilson av.
Feeney, Patrick J.	125	Belmont st.	Freeto, John F. Jr.	16	Bartlett rd.
Felker, G. C.	10	Marlboro st.	Freman, Hiram		Prospect st.
Fermia, Nicholas	32	Grant av.	French, Joseph B.	154	Beech st.
Fenwick, Ernest T.	30	Goden st.	French, William C.	10	Hillside ter.
Fenwick, Frank A.	30	Goden st.	Frenning, John E.	35	Clover st.
Ferguson, Robert R.	20	Wilson av.	Friedel, Herman H.	54	Thomas st.
Fillebrown, Warren A.		Concord av.	Frink, Arthur H.		Pleasant st.
Fillmore, John M.	68	Dartmouth st.	Frost, Albert H.	307	Pleasant st.
Fillmore, Millard	55	Sycamore st.	Frost, Chas. A.	301	Pleasant st.
Finlay, Charles W.	14	Blake st.	Frost, Everett A.	280	Pleasant st.
Finn, John V.	11	Myrtle st.	Frost, Henry	289	Pleasant st.
Finnegan, Thos.	7	Marion rd.	Frost, Henry E.		Pleasant st.
Fisher, Frank	11	Marion rd.	Frost, Irving B.	306	Pleasant st.
Fisher, Harry P.	334	Pleasant st.	Frost, J. Fred	480	Pleasant st.

ALPHABETICAL LIST OF POLLS.—*Con.*

NAME.	NO.	STREET.	NAME.	NO.	STREET.
Frost, Sylvester C.	308	Lake st.	Gordon, Elbridge W.		Pleasant st.
Frost, Walter E.	312	Pleasant st.	Gordon, George K.	20	Whitcomb st.
Frost, Walter L.	312	Pleasant st.	Gordon, Ira H.	47	Harriet av.
Frye, Winthrop B.	27	Park rd.	Gorham, Alfred M.	5	Pearl st.
Fuessel, George G.	45	Payson rd.	Gorham, Nathaniel T.	5	Pearl st.
Fulginiti, Dominico	140	White st.	Gorham, William M.	5	Pearl st.
Fuller, Alfred C.	423	Belmont st.	Gosewisch, Frederick A.L.	9	Maple ter.
Fuller, Frank	57	Marlboro st.	Goss, George F.	562	Trapelo rd.
Fuller, Ralph E.	45	Dartmouth st.	Gould, Charles H.	28	Oak av.
Fuller, Royal	60	Thomas st.	Gould, Ernest L.	179	Belmont st.
Fulton, John E.	21	Davis rd.	Gould, William H.	789	Belmont st.
Furlong, William J.	15	Davis st.	Gowan, Alonzo	600	Trapelo rd.
Furniss, William E.	30	Orchard st.	Gowey, Fred L.	156	Beech st.
Galatti, Joseph	15	Grant av.	Graham, Geo. D.		Pleasant st.
Galgano, Joseph	12	Baker st.	Grant, Edward F.	12	Midland st.
Gallagher, Hughie	137	Belmont st.	Grant, John F.	9	Agassiz av.
Gallagher, John	33	Grove st.	Grant, William H.	12	Midland st.
Gallagher, William	33	Grove st.	Grassie, W. S.	92	Bartlett av.
Gallagher, William A.	33	Grove st.	Gray, Bernard C.	25	Marion rd.
Galvin, John	121	Belmont st.	Gray, James	7	Ericsson st.
Galvin, Mortimer	121	Belmont st.	Gray, Joseph	5	B st.
Gano, Seth T.	70	Clark st.	Gray, Joseph M.	69	Grove st.
Garber, Robert A.	63	Hull st.	Gray, Norman A.	7	Townsend rd.
Gardener, Alfred H.	61	Marlboro st.	Gray, Robert W.	51	Oak av.
Gardener, Andrew J.	152	Beech st.	Grellish, Patrick	98	Grove st.
Gardener, John	off	Concord av.	Green, Albert R.		Stone rd.
Gardiner, Raynor		Hillcrest rd.	Green, William	60	Lexington st.
Gardner, James	143	Belmont st.	Greene, Walter	17	Springfield st.
Garner, William	26	Ridge rd.	Greenwood, Geo. W.	34	Cottage st.
Garfield, Walter T.	229	Belmont st.	Greer, Thomas A.	491	Belmont st.
Garland, Charles A.	7	Exeter st.	Grieano, Nicholas	104	Waverley st.
Garland, Herbert	682	Concord av.	Griffin, Timothy	194	Waverley st.
Garland, James B.	682	Concord av.	Griffin, William	31	Brighton st.
Garrity, Geo. A.	100	White st.	Griffith, Norman H.	36	Hawthorn st.
Gass, James S.	78	Spring st.	Grillo, John		Alexander av.
Gay, Harry D.	497	Common st.	Grimes, Arthur G.	54	School st.
George, Edwin R.	100	White st.	Grimes, J. Henry	54	School st.
Gerace, Frank	140	White st.	Grimes, William	54	School st.
Gervais, Stanislas	172	Beech st.	Grimes, William F. Jr.	54	School st.
Gethro, George W.	4	Marion rd.	Grinnell, Elmer N.		Pleasant st.
Gibb, Thomas R. P.	27	Goden st.	Grotjohan, Philip F.	62	Pine st.
Gibson, Henry T.	45	Lexington st.	Gruhn, Adolph A.	23	Oxford av.
Gibson, Thomas H.	45	Lexington st.	Gruhn, Fred W.	23	Oxford av.
Gigger, Emory W.	20	Wilson av.	Guertin, Augustus	15	Woodland st.
Gildea, James	33	Grove st.	Gullifer, Harry	125	Pine st.
Giles, John R.	32	Oak av.	Gullifer, William H.	125	Pine st.
Gill, Harold L.	230	Payson rd.	Gunn, Ernest D. B.	40	Alma av.
Gilpatrick, Chas.	123	Alexander av.	Gunning, Thomas		Creeley rd.
Ginesti, Dominic	408	Trapelo rd.	Gustafson, Emanuel	11	Harriet av.
Gitelson, Hyman	34	Maple st.	Gustafson, Fred	11	Harriet av.
Glading, Wilson	55	Dartmouth st.	Gustafson, Gunner S.	11	Harriet av.
Gladwin, C. A.	92	Payson rd.	Gustafson, John F.	50	Oxford av.
Glaser, Frank	361	Trapelo rd.	Gustafson, Samuel	11	Harriet av.
Gleason, John J.	263	Waverley st.	Hackett, Francis	48	Creeley rd.
Gonean, Alphonse A. J.	12	Frederick st.	Hagerty, Eugene		Drew rd.
Goodwin, Elisha	117	White st.	Haigh, William	27	Cutter st.
Goodwin, Gilbert A.	50	Lexington st.	Hale, Brownell W.	125	White st.
Goodwin, Harry	7	Vincent av.	Hale, Charles E.	125	White st.
Goodwin, Morris H.	10	Cutter st.	Hale, Wm. Charles		Pleasant st.
Goodwin, Sam H.	10	Cutter st.	Hall, Eben A.	45	Pine st.
Gordon, Albert B.	20	Whitcomb st.	Hall, Harrison B.	400	Trapelo rd.

ALPHABETICAL LIST OF POLLS.—*Con.*

NAME.	NO.	STREET.	NAME.	NO.	STREET.
Hall, Harry	25	Falmouth st.	Hennessey, John	36	Maple st.
Hall, Harold, T.	31	Pine st.	Hennessey, John T.	7	Agassiz av.
Hall, Malcolm B.	141	Lexington st.	Henry, Danford T.	219	Lexington st
Hall, Robert H.	141	Lexington st.	Henry, J. Wilbert		Prospect st.
Hall, Wesley G.	141	Lexington st.	Henshaw, Chas. S.	231	Belmont st.
Hamblen, Clarence	9	Marion rd.	Hernesz, Loratte	40	Baker st.
Hamm, John D.	227	White st.	Hernon, Patrick T.		Church st. p
Hammer, Chas. D.	15	Kilburn rd.	Herrick, Robert W.	229	Belmont st.
Handrahan, Raymond A.	213	White st.	Heuser, Emil	95	Beech st.
Hands, James	392	Concord av.	Heustis, Lancaster H.		Heustis rd.
Hanf, Adolf	19	Springfield st.	Heustis, Warren H.		Heustis rd.
Hankard, Edward J.	63	Hull st.	Higgins, Bernard	198	Waverley st.
Hankin, Chas. A.	30	Grove st.	Highley, Philip.	10	Bartlett rd.
Hanley, Chas. C.	61	Unity av.	Highley, Robert	10	Bartlett rd.
Hanson, Martin P.	93	Beech st.	Hill, Alfred C.	400	Pleasant st.
Hanson, Michael	13	Ash st.	Hill, Amos E.		Hill rd.
Hanson, William C.	395	Belmont st.	Hill, Clarence O.	400	Pleasant st.
Hapgood, Richard	642	Pleasant st.	Hill, Edward E.	25	Marion rd.
Harding, Frederick	36	Church st.	Hill, J. Willard	400	Pleasant st.
Harper, Frank W.	51	Alma av.	Hill, Willard M.	400	Pleasant st.
Harrington, Albert D.	146	Beech st.	Hill, William M.	57	Berwick st.
Harrington, Albert H.	146	Beech st.	Hilton, Frank H.	20	Cushing av.
Harrington, Chas. S.	158	Beech st.	Hilton, John P.	20	Cushing av.
Harrington, James	61	Grove st.	Hilton, Everett S.	27	Cushing av.
Harrington, John J.	37	Wilson av.	Hinckley Crandall H.	208	White st.
Harris, Fred B.	122	Brighton st.	Hines, Bartley	2	Exeter st.
Harris, George A.	27	Willow st.	Hines, Thomas R.		Trapelo rd.
Harris, Harry		Benjamin rd.	Hinton, John R.	45	Lexington st
Harris, Judson I.	7	Agassiz av.	Hittinger, Charles F.	375	School st.
Harris, Thomas F.	247	Waverley st.	Hittinger, Edward K.	45	Elm st.
Harrison, Benjamin S.		Church st. pl.	Hittinger, Jacob	216	Common st.
Harrison, John T.		Church st. pl.	Hittinger, Richard	45	Elm st.
Harrod, W. T.	11	Cutter st.	Hoar, Maurice,	340	Lake st.
Hart, John P.	20	Pine st.	Hoch, Theodore A.	165	Mill st.
Harty, John F.	17	Leonard st.	Hodgdon, Frank M.	245	Washington
Harty, William	17	Leonard st.	Hogan, Francis S.		Pleasant st.
Harvey, Wendell T.	113	White st.	Hollander, Wilkie B.	17	Lawndale st.
Haskell, George H.	20	Moraine st.	Hollis, John T.	61	Marlboro st.
Haskins, Fred	220	Lexington st.	Holmburg, John	29	Falmouth st.
Hatch, A. John	25	Centre av.	Holmes, Fred L.	211	Lexington st
Hatch, Alvah L.	25	Centre av.	Holmes, William H.	85	Beech st.
Hatch, Edward W.	247	Waverley st.	Holscher, Edwin	214	Lexington s
Hatch, Ernest L.	25	Centre av.	Holscher, Harry	214	Lexington s
Hatch, Simon D.	25	Centre av.	Holscher, Henry A.	214	Lexington s
Hatch, Simon D. Sr.	23	Centre av.	Holt, Rollin L.	232	Washington
Hathaway, LeRoy	44	Waverley st.	Holton, Cheney J.	35	Moraine st.
Haviland, W. J.	29	Wilson av.	Homer, Sydney M.	65	Oak av.
Hawkes, A. J.	52	Marlboro st.	Honeth, Gustaf G.	25	Creeley rd.
Hawkes, Nathan	56	Marlboro st.	Hood, James H.	211	Belmont st.
Hawthorne, Robert	72	Trapelo rd.	Hopkins, Raymond A.	5	Concord av.
Hayden, Frank A.	84	Lexington st.	Horn, Alvin H.	rear 343	Pleasant st
Hayes, Lloyd B.		Blake st.	Horne, Geoffrey	602	Belmont st.
Hayes, William	146	Trapelo rd.	Horne, Richard B.	146	Trapelo rd.
Hazelton, Charles	21	Francis st.	Hough, Arthur E.	20	Moraine st.
Heckman, Raymond H.	50	Waverley st.	Hough, Charles G.	59	Common st.
Hedlund, True	68	Dartmouth st.	Houghton, Frank G.	194	Common st.
Hellen, John	57	Grove st.	Houlahan, Charles H.	22	Waverley st.
Hellen, Oscar	72	Oxford av.	Howard, Francis, J.	6	Orchard st.
Hellen, Rudolph	72	Oxford av.	Howard, John	2	Worcester st
Henley, Joseph A.	26	Marion rd.	Howden, Charles	439	Pleasant st.
Hennessy, James F.	33	Wilson av.	Howe, James A.	536	Pleasant st.

NAME.	NO.	STREET.	NAME.	NO.	STREET.
Howe, James A.	536	Pleasant st.	Johnson, Carl E.	73	Marlboro st.
Howe, Percy R.	536	Pleasant st.	Johnson, Carl W.	24	Falmouth st.
Howell, Sidney K.		Pleasant st.	Johnson, Charles	17	Park rd.
Howes, Benjamin L.	67	Oak st.	Johnson, Christenson	138	Beech st.
Howes, Clifton, A.	41	Pine st.	Johnson, Daniel C.	24	Falmouth st.
Hoyer, Ernest	588	Trapelo rd.	Johnson, Emil	178	Waverley st.
Hoyer, Fritz		Pleasant st.	Johnson, Frank	75	Lexington st.
Hoyt, Henry A.	233	Common st.	Johnson, Frank W.	45	Marlboro st.
Hoyt, Samuel W.		Stone rd.	Johnson, Frederick	53	Thomas st.
Hubbard, Perley O.		Irving st.	Johnson, George	58	Marlboro st.
Hubbard, William M.	35	Agassiz av.	Johnson, Harris S.	13	Maple ter.
Huddy. Frederick L.		Townsend rd.	Johnson, Hugh	248	Mill st.
Hudson, Harry W.	21	Pine st.	Johnson, John	42	Grove st.
Hughes, Chester C.	6	Moraine st.	Johnson, Julius E.	19	Concord av.
Hughes, Philip K.	6	Moraine st.	Johnson, Kimball		David rd.
Hull, Chester B.		Bartlett av.	Johnson, Liles		Creeley rd.
Hull, Chester A.	235	Belmont st.	Johnson, Matts	16	Marlboro st.
Hunt, Chandler	721	Pleasant st.	Johnson, Olof	3	Falmouth st.
Hunt, Fred O.	215	Belmont st.	Johnson, Werner E.	175	Beech st.
Huntoun, Lawrence		Pleasant st.	Johnston Albert H.	45	Marion rd.
Hurley, John	18	Cross st.	Johnston, Andrew N.	45	Willow st.
Hurley, John H.	26	Cross st.	Johnston, William A.	35	Hillside ter.
Hurley, Patrick	26	Cross st.	Jolin, Simon G.	45	Hull st.
Hurley, Patrick C.	20	Cross st.	Jones, Charles L.	off	Concord av.
Hurley, Patrick T.	26	Cross st.	Jones, George H.	37	Marion rd.
Hurley, Peter		Pleasant st.	Jones, Lewis A.	29	Falmouth st.
Hurley, William J.	20	Cross st.	Jones, St. Clair	24	Orchard st.
Huse, C. P.	21	Pine st.	Jones, Walter F.	21	Goden st.
Husband, Alexander P.	35	Cedar rd.	Jordan, Everard W.	30	Oak st.
Husband, John	35	Cedar rd.	Jordan, Joseph	40	Myrtle st.
Husband, Robert G.	35	Cedar rd.	Jordan, Raymond W.	30	Oak st.
Huston, Charles E.	352	Pleasant st.	Joyce, William H.	15	Marlboro st.
Hutchinson, James	21	Lawndale st.	Kakefiro, Bastin		David rd.
Igo, Bernard F.	85	Cross st.	Kanaly, Frank M.	26	Park rd.
Igo, Peter	85	Cross st.	Kanaly, Morris E.	16	Park rd.
Igo, William A.	85	Cross st.	Kanaly, Paul J.	16	Park rd.
Ingram, Lester W.	146	Waverley st.	Kaplan, George	105	Beech st.
Irving, Samuel R.	26	Huron av.	Kearns, Edward J.	17	Maple st.
Jack, Horatio	624	Pleasant st.	Kearns, Joseph	88	Beech st.
Jack, William A.	77	Beech st.	Kearns, Michael	88	Beech st.
Jackson, Frank	161	Washington st	Kedian, James E.	34	Cushing av.
Jackson, Frank H.	31	Moraine st.	Keefe, Michael	16	Cross st.
Jackson, Phillip S.	161	Washington st	Keefe, Patrick	493	School st.
Jacobs, Percival D.	12	Moore st.	Keefe, Thomas	39	Thomas st.
Jacobson, Fridolf M.		David rd.	Keefe, Timothy	39	Thomas st.
Jacobson, Rev. Henning		David rd.	Keegan, James F.	18	Chandler st.
Jacobson, Joseph H.		David rd.	Keegan, William H.	16	Church st.
James, William H.		Hillside ter.	Keenan, Francis R.	300	Brighton st.
Jameson, Claude S.	132	White st.	Keenan, James A.	300	Brighton st.
Jameson, Winthrop S.	52	Lawndale st.	Keenan, Patrick J.	253	Waverley st.
Jarvis, Charles, A.	179	Belmont st.	Kelley, James W.	161	Beech st.
Jaynes, James	410	Trapelo rd.	Kelley, James W.		Trapelo rd.
Jefferson, John R.	11	Ash st.	Kelly, Fred	11	Davis rd.
Jenks, Simeon	51	White st.	Kelly, Herbert L.	200	Common st.
Jenney, Charles	46	Centre av.	Kelly, John J.	73	Grove st.
Johnson, Allan	66	Dartmouth st.	Kelly, Thomas A.	25	Pine st.
Johnson, August	52	Creeley rd.	Kellog, Alfred S.	6	Hawthorn st.
Johnson, Agustus B.	48	Dartmouth st.	Kellog, Arthur J.	29	Wilson av.
Johnson, Axel	20	Ericsson st.	Kelso, Robert W.	24	Clover st.
Johnson, Axel	35	Concord av.	Kendall, Arthur E.	29	Winter st.
Johnson, Carl	1	Marion rd.	Kendall, Arthur S.	25	Common st.

ALPHABETICAL LIST OF POLLS.—*Con.*

NAME.	NO.	STREET.	NAME.	NO.	STREET.
Kendall, Charles P.		Wellington st.	Lamson, Henry H.	61	Marlboro st.
Kendall, Francis H.	47	Clark st.	Lamson, Howard E.	181	Belmont st.
Kendall, Francis H.	25	Common st.	Landall, Abel E.	138	Beech st.
Kendall, George	178	Mill st.	Landall, Charles R.	138	Beech st.
Kendall, George A.	178	Mill st.	Landall, E. Lawrence	52	Burnham st.
Kendall, G. Fred	146	Mill st.	Landall, Phillip A.	30	Ridge rd.
Kendall, J. Henry	178	Mill st.	Landall, Simon P.	138	Beech st.
Kendall, John H.	25	Common st.	Landregan, Patrick J.	23	Park rd.
Kendall, Paul	25	Common st.	Lane, Josiah F.	60	Oak av.
Kendall, Walter S.	16	Holt st.	Langley, W. F.	60	Sycamore st.
Kennedy, Andrew	4	Thomas st.	Lansil, Earl F.	33	Burnham st.
Kennedy, John A.	142	Waverley st.	Larrabee, Bertram C.	6	Ericsson st.
Kennedy, John J.	27	Leonard st.	Larrabee, Everett C.	107	Sycamore st.
Kennedy, Ross M.		Pleasant st.	Larabee, Howard B.	107	Sycamore st.
Kennedy, William J.	1026	Pleasant st.	Larrabee, Robert B.	107	Sycamore st.
Kennedy, William S.		Old Concord rd.	Larson, Carl		Pleasant st.
Kenny, John	5	Falmouth st.	Laspada, Antonio	17	Grant av.
Kenny, Michael	102	Brighton st.	Latimer, Elbert S.	22	Marion rd.
Kenrick, Bowman H.	52	Alexander av.	Latimer, Hugh	185	White st.
Kenrick, Oscar B.	52	Alexander av.	Lawrence, Alden L.	610	Trapelo rd.
Kenrick, Walter H.	52	Alexander av.	Lawrence, Archie W.		Pleasant st.
Kerrigan, John	103	Beech st.	Lawson, Hans L.	43	Marlboro st.
Kerrigan, John		Concord av.	Lawton, Fred H.	122	Beech st.
Kessler, William		Baker st.	Leacy, Martin	61	Waverley st.
Keville, William J.	174	School st.	Leahy, Martin W.	off	Concord av.
Kewer, Howard	16	Hawthorn st.	Leavitt, F. C.	87	Pine st.
Kewer, William J.	19	Hawthorn st.	LeBlanc, William	16	Moraine st.
Kidder, Melvin	12	Park rd.	Lee, Alphonse	310	Brighton st.
Kierstead, George A.	11	Davis rd.	Lee, S. Southard	59	Berwick st.
Kihlberg, Karl A.	75	Marlboro st.	Lee, Walter N.	219	Belmont st.
Kilburn, Austin S.	223	Belmont st.	Lehr, Hugo	17	Park rd.
Kilpatrick, Charles W.	17	Sycamore st.	Leighton, Rual J.		Pleasant st.
Kimball, Clarence L.	17	Pine st.	Leland, Clarence E.	51	Maple st.
Kimball, Samuel A.		Pleasant st.	Leonard, Fred C.	21	Sunnyside pl
Kimball, Thomas F.	331	Waverley st.	Leonard, John F.	21	Sunnyside pl
Kindahl, Frederick	24	Marlboro st.	Leonard, Wm. T.	11	Oak av.
King, Arthur J.	22	Falmouth st.	Lettiere, Dominick	9	B st.
King, Charles M.	57	Grove st.	Lettiere, Rocky	9	B st.
King, Frank L.	11	Lexington st.	Levao, Nino	65	Walnut st.
King, Gilbert A.	46	Thomas st.	Lever, Geo. W.	33	Chandler st.
King, Melvin E.	223	White st.	Levin, Zelim	13	Oxford av.
Kinread, Wm. R.	105	Sycamore st.	Levitt, Harry W.	55	Berwick st.
Kirschten, Frederick W.	9	Ericsson st.	Lewald, Aswald		Pleasant st.
Knapp, Frank S.	24	Cutter st.	Lewis, Arthur F.	11	Park rd.
Knibb, Albert E.	17	Harriet av.	Lewis, Agustus	20	Cambridge st
Knight, John W.	47	Hawthorn st.	Lewis, Ellsworth M.	65	Marlboro st.
Knirsch, John	7	Concord av.	Libbey, Joseph E.	230	White st.
Knudsen, Axel E.	223	Belmont st.	Lietz, Carl	50	Chandler st.
Krause, Herman H.	22	Exeter st.	Lindley, F. B.	22	Park rd.
Kuhn, David P.	15	Marion rd.	Lindstrowm, Frank O.	16	Ericsson st.
Kurtz, Charles C.		Kilburn rd.	Linscott, Robert N.	25	Wilson av.
Kylie, Morris	76	Cross st.	Lippe, Raoul J.	101	Beech st.
LaBonte, Frank N.	2	Chenery ter.	Lisano, Maurice	5	A st.
LaFlamme, T. Leo	397	Belmont st.	Lister, Robert N.	20	Hillside ter.
Lagerblade, August A.	56	Oxford av.	Little, Richard		Walnut st.
Lahaie, David	17	Underwood st.	Little, Waldo F.	46	Burnham st.
Lahty, Enoch I.	582	Pleasant st.	Littlejohn, Albert V.	12	Francis st.
Lalor, Edmond I.	26	Park rd.	Littlejohn, George J.	12	Francis st.
Lambrie, George	52	Dartmouth st.	Littlejohn, James	12	Francis st.
Lamkin, W. R.	785	Belmont st.	Livermore, Charles E.	53A	Dartmouth s
Lamont, Raymond	145	Belmont st.	Locke, Edwin A.	25	Somerset st.

ALPHABETICAL LIST OF POLLS.—*Con.*

NAME.	NO.	STREET.	NAME.	NO.	STREET.
Locke, Frank M.	61	Waverley st.	MacAuliffe, Florence F.	175	Beech st.
Locke, Galen L.	53	Cushing av.	MacDonald, Albert J.		Stone rd.
Locke, George S.	53	Cushing av.	MacDonald, John		Stone rd.
Locke, George T.	634	Pleasant st.	MacDonald, John J.	62	Marlboro st.
Locke, George W.	631	Pleasant st.	Macgregor, Daniel	49	Marion rd.
Locke, James E.	575	Pleasant st.	Mack, Fred F.	346	Trapelo rd.
Locke, John A.	25	Somerset st.	Mack, John H.	70	Oakley rd.
Locke, Isaac B.	561	Pleasant st.	Mackay, Edgar F.	811	Belmont st.
Locke, Isaac H.	561	Pleasant st.	Mackay, Hector	811	Belmont st.
Locke, Melvin	53	Cushing av.	Mackenzie, Fredwith R.	25	Falmouth st.
Locke, Richard B.		Howells rd.	Mackenzie, James	20	Moraine st.
Locke, William H.	59	Cushing av.	MacKenzie, John G.	83	Beech st.
Locke, William H.	561	Pleasant st.	MacLane, Vinal B.	61	Dartmouth st.
Locke, William I.	61	Leonard st.	MacLean, Archibald	21	Falmouth st.
Lockhart, Alexander C.	70	School st.	MacLennan, John	50	Dartmouth st.
Lockhart, Edward C.	18	Marion rd.	MacLeod, Alexander	16	Church st.
Loftus, James F.	31	Brighton st.	Macolini, Frank	48	Grant av.
Loftus, John	31	Brighton st.	Macomber, Eugene T.	42	Burnham st.
Logan, Crayton	38	Cottage st.	Maffei, Michael	42	Grant av.
Logan, George		Pleasant st.	Magnuson, Bernard	25	Creeley rd.
Logan, James R.	570	Trapelo rd.	Magnuson, Bror E.	403	Trapelo rd.
Lomadico, Michael	36	Grant av.	Magnuson, Eric	49	Marlboro st.
LoMeyers, Joseph	104	Waverley st.	Magoon, Henry E.	251	Mill st.
Lonergan, Frank E.	10	Ericsson st.	Maguire, Edward		off Pleasant st.
Lonergan, James M.	10	Ericsson st.	Maguire, James J.	12	Woodland st.
Long, Albert B.	32	Willow st.	Maguire, John	55	Thomas st.
Long, Alfred H.	80	Washington st	Maguire, John F.	19	Ash st.
Long, Edward	28	Grove st.	Maguire, Patrick		off Pleasant st.
Long, James F.	28	Grove st.	Maguire, Patrick	35	Oak st.
Long, Jeremiah J.	28	Grove st.	Mahan, James	17	Trowbridge st.
Longden, Joseph	48	Grove st.	Mahegan, Albert F.	59	Berwick st.
Longridge, Thomas S.	54	Oakley rd.	Mahiedas, John		Pleasant st.
Loomer, Ashly	221	Belmont st.	Mahoney, Daniel J.	653	Concord av.
Loomer, Frank L.	143	Sycamore sr.	Mahoney, Henry F.	56	Agassiz av.
Loomer, Guy	2	Park rd.	Mahoney, Robert V.	247	Waverley st.
Loomer, P. F.	22	Park rd.	Mahoney, William F.		White st.
Looney, Edward J.	275	Waverley st.	Major, Arthur H.	26	Agassiz av.
Looney, James	269	Waverley st.	Major, Alfred E.	26	Agassiz av.
Looney, Timothy F.	271	Waverley st.	Malenfant, Joseph F.	36	Jeanette av.
Lord, Frederick T.	35	Pine st.	Malensten Ernest A.	59	Berwick st.
Loring, Bentley E.	114	White st.	Malmsten, Chas.	45	Marlboro st.
Loring, Frank E.	7	Oak av.	Malmstrom, Nils	6	Worcester st.
Loring, Joshua	114	White st.	Malmstrom, Vitalis	6	Worcester st.
Lothrop, James F.	100	White st.	Malone, Frank	78	Spring st.
Loud, John A.	323	Waverley st.	Malone, Fred	25	Creeley rd.
Loumos, Anast	25	Maple st.	Mamelian, Paul	489	Trapelo rd.
Lowrance, John W.	13	Pine st.	Mann, David W.	34	Jeanette av.
Lowrington, Richard W.		Pleasant st.	Mann, Wallace R.	159	Beech st.
Lowry, Kierson J.	90	Pine st.	Mannix, Timothy J.		Huron av.
Lufkin, Edwin F.		Irving st.	Manson, Warren	212	Lexington st.
Lundberg, William A.	20	Ericsson st.	Marando, Patsy	9	B st.
Lunsford, Maurice P.	1	Spinney ter.	Marchmond, Chas. M.	99	Beech st.
Luscia,	138	Sycamore st.	Marean, Henry E.	57	Payson rd.
Luszcz, Martin		Benjamin rd.	Marenaen, Nelson	52	Dartmouth st.
Lynch, Edward F.		Pleasant st.	Marie, Frank W.	37	Moraine st.
Lynch, Elwood N.	403	Trapelo rd.	Marks, Thomas W.	147	Beech st.
Lynch, Frank K.	281	Payson rd.	Marsh, Ernest V.	22	Ericsson st.
Lynch, Norman R.	403	Trapelo rd.	Marsh, Henry L.	20	Moraine st.
Lynch, Walter H.	403	Trapelo rd.	Marsh, William P.	172	Lexington st.
Lyons, John S.	75	Lexington st.	Marshall, Anbury M.	39	Harriet av.
Lyons, Patrick	75	Lexington st.	Martinolich, Nicholas	61	Grove st.

ALPHABETICAL LIST OF POLLS.—*Con.*

NAME.	NO.	STREET.	NAME.	NO.	STREET.
Mason, Alban A.	21	Fairview av.	McKisson, Arthur		Pleasant st.
Mason, George E.	56	Agassiz av.	McLaskey, Miles E.	616	Trapelo rd.
Mason, J. Munroe	41	Oak st.	McLaughlin, Dennis		Bartlett av.
Mason, Nathaniel	21	Fairview av.	McLaughlin, Joseph F.	10	Francis st.
Mason, Ralph T.	33	Goden st.	McLean, Arthur	10	Moraine st.
Mason, Theodore	33	Goden st.	McLean, Arthur W.	1	Stone rd.
Mason, Wendell F.	3	Oxford av.	McLean, Malcolm Allen		Pleasant st.
Massey, Harry D.	15	Park rd.	McLearn, Arthur H.	349	Trapelo rd.
Massey, William T.	24	Oxford av.	McMahon, Ambrose	26	Agassiz av.
Matheson, C. B.	50	Oxford av.	McMahon, Patrick T.	226	Waverley st.
Matheson, J. C.	50	Oxford av.	McMurdie, Orgin A.	23	Francis st.
Mattsson, Victor	23	Park rd.	McNamee, A. Percy	89	Grove st.
May, John J.		Pleasant st.	McNamee, David	407	Trapelo rd.
Maynard, Elmer W.	38	Lexington st.	McNamee, John R.	407	Trapelo rd.
Mazzeo, Anthony	5	B st.	McNamee, William A.	89	Grove st.
McAleer, Dearborn J.	365	Trapelo rd.	McNaught, Arthur J.	50	School st.
McAleer, Thomas G.	365	Trapelo rd.	McNealy, Francis	17	Exeter st.
McAllister, John J.	75	Beech st.	NcNeil, Edmund J.	346	Trapelo rd.
McArdle, James W.	38	Oakley rd.	McNeil, John	392	Concord av.
McBride, James	103	Beech st.	McNeil, John E.	12	Cottage st.
McBride, John	103	Beech st.	McNeil, John H.	25	Cutter st.
McBride, John	75	Lexington st.	McNeil, Prescott	392	Concord av.
McCaig, Joseph	81	Concord av.	McNulty, Edward	62	Thomas st.
McCaig, Robert E.	81	Concord av.	McPartland, James	35	Concord av.
McCarragher, Thomas	75	Lexington st.	McPhail, Murdock	218	Lake st.
McCarthy, Charles E.	67	White st.	McQuaid, James	6	Thomas st.
McCarthy, Edmund	480	Concord av.	McReavy, H. L.	21	Springfield st.
McCarthy, Edward H.	117	Belmont st.	McRoberts, William N.		Maple st.
McCarthy, John F.	159	Alexander av.	Mead, F. Walton Jr.	29	Wilson av.
McCarthy, John V.	242	Trapelo rd.	Mead, John H.	296	Concord av.
McConnell, Charles W.	610	Trapelo rd.	Mead, John H.	rear 343	Pleasant st.
McCormick, John	25	Thomas st.	Mead, P. Henry	296	Concord av.
McCoy, Hugh A.	87	Pine st.	Mead, Michael	off 343	Pleasant st.
McCreary, Lewis S.	315	Belmont st.	Mee, Patrick	10	Oxford av.
McCuen, Fred J.	14	Pine st.	Meehan, George	43	Maple st.
McCuen, Walter C.	17	Pine st.	Meek, Samuel	24	Oxford av.
McCulloch, David		Pleasant st.	Meek, Spratt M.	41	Unity av.
McCutcheon, James E.	36	Grove st.	Meharg, Robert R.	22	Park rd.
McDermott, Joseph H.		Henry st.	Meisel, Edward J.	off	Concord av.
McDermott, Michael E.	43	Hawthorn st.	Meisel, Fred J.	off	Concord av.
McDermott, Timothy F.	46	Cottage st.	Melanson, Joseph E.	4	Cambridge st.
McDermott, T. J.	43	Hawthorn st.	Melanson, Charles	122	Waverley st.
McDevitt, James		Pleasant st.	Melanson, Delby C.	122	Waverley st.
McDonald, Daniel	43	Concord av.	Melanson, Theodore J.	122	Waverley st.
McDonald, James J.	202	Waverley st.	Melino, Andrew	9	Underwood st.
McDonald, Thomas H.	54	Marlboro st.	Mellett, Patrick	333	Concord av.
McDonald, William	618	Pleasant st.	Melville, Samuel P.	44	Wilson av.
McDonald, William W.	618	Pleasant st.	Menard, Joseph	68	Thomas st.
McGinnis, Andrew	293	Concord av.	Mera, William A.	61	Dartmouth st
McGinnis, Charles J.	293	Concord av.	Mercer, Alfred		Pleasant st.
McGinnis, Patrick H.	293	Concord av.	Mercer, Nathan	11	Lexington st.
McGinty, John V.	126	Sycamore st.	Merriam, C. R.	86	Payson rd.
McGlue, Hugh P.	27	School st.	Merrill, Allyne L.	21	Hillside ter.
McIlroy, John	54	Dartmouth st.	Merrill, Fletcher D.	27	School st.
McIntosh, Walter H.	163	Belmont st.	Merrow, Charles F.	39	Willow st.
McKay, Robert F.	34	Wilson av.	Mershon, Stephen L.	27	Cutter st.
McKee, Fred W.	14	Pine st.	Metcalf, Albert S.	21	Park rd.
McKeen, Leslie R.	95	Grove st.	Metcalf, Fred	85	Concord av.
McKenn, Henry	321	Brighton st.	Metcalf, Raymond	85	Concord av.
McKenzie, Forbes	76	Lexington st.	Mickmerry, Thomas		Pleasant st.
McKenzie, Geo. L.	76	Lexington st.	Middleton, Ben	107	Beech st,

Alphabetical List of Polls.—*Con.*

Name.	No.	Street.	Name.	No.	Street.
Miller, Geo. H.		Hill rd.	Mullen, William B.	23	Oakley rd.
Miller, James	69	Waverley st.	Mullett, Fred A.	37	Wilson av.
Miller, John F.	69	Waverley st.	Mulrey, Patrick	307	Belmont st.
Miller, Joseph	115	Waverley st.	Mulvihill, William	108	Sycamore st.
Miller, Walter J.	15	Exeter st.	Munday, Willard E.	229	White st.
Millerick, John	66	Spring st.	Munn, Eugene E.	227	White st.
Millerick, Patrick	24	Cross st.	Munroe, Alexander		Pleasant st.
Millett, John	331	Concord av.	Murdoch, Joseph	53	Harriet av.
Millette, Francis L.	15	Woodland st.	Murfa, Michael	40	Grant av.
Mills, Charles	16	Harriet av.	Murphy, Andrew J.	47	Agassiz av.
Millward, Albert J.	40	Thayer rd.	Murphy, Daniel J.	172	Waverley st.
Minty, Albion	48	Bartlett av.	Murphy, Daniel L.	2	Cherry st.
Minty, Keywood C.	38	Alma av.	Murphy, Dennis	17	Maple ter.
Moffat, Albert S.	6	Springfield st.	Murphy, Edward	61	Sycamore sr.
Moltman, William J.	70	Oakley rd.	Murphy, Frank E.	149	Waverley st.
Monaghan, Edward W.		Wellington st.	Murphy, James A.	58	Oxford av.
Mondello, Joseph	45	Trowbridge st.	Murphy, Patrick B.	7	Agassiz av.
Moody, Ralph L.	75	Marlboro st.	Murphy, Patrick J.		Henry st.
Moore, Geo. E.	81	Lexington st.	Murphy, Thomas W.	149	Waverley st.
Moore, H. S.	68	Payson rd.	Murphy, William	off	Concord av.
Moore, Mark	8	Alma av.	Murray, John D.	50	Falmouth st.
Moore, W. H.	59	Chandler st.	Murray, William H.	9	Davis rd.
Moorehead, Geo. A.	146	Beech st.	Murtaugh, William J.	16	Davis rd.
Moran, Peter		Pleasant st.	Napoli, Antonio	59	Grant av.
Morash, Charles E.	242	White st.	Narbut, Walter S.	15	Baker st.
Morash, C. Ross	236	White st.	Natale, Laneia	7	A st.
Morash, Fred	52	Oakley rd.	Nazzaro, Joseph	59	Baker st.
Morette, Lawrence	15	Concord av.	Neal, Joseph E.		Pleasant st.
Morgan, Edward D.	31	Moraine st.	Nelson, Carl E.	15	Exeter st.
Morgan, John C.	53	Dartmouth st.	Nelson, Olaf	17	Marlboro st.
Morgan, Otto F.	52	Marlboro st.	Neptune, Richard	138	Waverley st.
Moriarty, Oscar F.	111	School st.	Nesie, Joe		David rd.
Morrill, Rex.	18	Cambridge st.	Nestor, Michael	50	Creeley rd.
Morrill, Chas. H.	365	Trapelo rd.	Newcomb, John W.	12	Burnham st.
Morrill, Winfred	365	Trapelo rd.	Newman, Christopher	14	Oxford av.
Morris, Harold W.	19	Francis st.	Newman, Edward F.	14	Oxford av.
Morrisey, John	335	Concord av.	Newman, Philip	23	Baker st.
Morrisey, John J.	123	Alexander av.	Nichols, Jonathan E.	151	Beech st.
Morrisey, John J. Jr.	335	Concord av.	Nichols, Patrick	27	Underwood st.
Morrison, James H.	33	Orchard st.	Nichols, William H.	9	Maple ter.
Morrison, Richard E.	6	Orchard st.	Nickerson, Edrick R.	58	Marlboro st.
Morrow, James L.	9	Ash st.	Nickerson, Geo. E.	58	Marlboro st.
Morrow, William J.	9	Ash st.	Nickerson, Mortimer	100	Trapelo rd.
Morrow, William W.	9	Ash st.	Nickerson, Samuel	52	Thomas st.
Morse, Charles F.	77	Pine st.	Nickerson, William A.	83	Lexington st.
Morse, C. Harry	20	Orchard st.	Niland, Martin	188	Waverley st.
Morse, Edward	28	Springfield st.	Nobriga, Chas. B.	72	Goden st.
Morse, Floyd B.	58	Dartmouth st.	Norris, Edmund H.	62	Oak av.
Morse, Harold		Pleasant st.	Norton, Arthur		Centre av.
Morse, James E.	28	Springfield st.	Norton, Harry E.		Trapelo rd.
Morse, James E. Jr.	28	Springfield st.	Norton, James E.	63	Fairview av.
Morse, John	15	Falmouth st.	Norton, Michael F.	431	School st.
Morton, Alfred M.	140	Spring st.	Norton, William M.	90	Trapelo rd.
Mosher, John L.	99	Beech st.	Norwood, Roscoe	183	Belmont st.
Moulton, Arthur C.		Belmont st.	Nutter, Chas. A.	77	Lexington st.
Moulton, David J.	26	Myrtle st.	Nystrom, John F.	323	Trapelo rd.
Mufficci, Michael	39	Baker st.	Nystrom, Karl N.	323	Trapelo rd.
Muirhead, James	9	Vincent av.	Oakes, John H.	34	Burnham st.
Mullen, Arthur J.	143	Belmont st.	O'Brien, Edward W.	7	Sunnyside pl.
Mullen, Raymond C.	23	Oakley rd.	O'Brien, John	26	Centre av.
Mullen, Seymour H.	11	Agassiz st.	O'Brien, John E.	26	Centre av.

ALPHABETICAL LIST OF POLLS.—*Con.*

NAME.	NO.	STREET.	NAME.	NO.	STREET.
O'Brien, John J.	10	Marlboro st.	Pasquale, Antro	9	Underwood st.
O'Brien, Joseph F.	26	Centre av.	Patrick, Harrie	23	Oxford av.
O'Brien, William	7	Sunnyside pl.	Patriquin, Burton	79	Lexington st.
O'Brien, William	26	Centre av.	Patterson, William H.	42	Wilson av.
O'Connell, John		Huron av.	Payne, Edward F.	10	Myrtle st.
O'Connor, Jeremiah	48	Thomas st.	Payson, Gilbert R.	545	Belmont st.
Odde, John A. L.	52	Willow st.	Peabody, John S.	27	Bartlett av.
O'Donnell, Michael	75	Lexington st.	Pearce, Aleck	73	Marlboro st.
O'Grady, Martin	42	Cottage st.	Pease, Alexander	25	Falmouth st.
O'Hara, James W.	4	Oak st.	Peckham, Albert B.	18	Holt st.
Oikemus, John	70	Grant av.	Peede, Loring G.		Common st.
Oken, Severin	339	Trapelo rd.	Peede, T. Richard		Common st.
Olive, Chas.	69	Marlboro st.	Peirce, Eugene E.	68	Leonard st.
Olive, Chas. R.	42	Marlboro st.	Peirce, Owen M.	626	Pleasant st.
Ollis, Harry		David rd.	Penn, Geo. J.	154	Beech st.
Olson, Alvin G.	40	Grove st.	Penney, Nicholas J.	136	Common st.
Olson, Carl	44	Pine st.	Perault, Arthur L.	34	Leonard st.
Olson, Chas.	9	Park rd.	Perault, John B.	34	Leonard st.
Olson, Edward	41	Marlboro st.	Perault, Peter P.	34	Leonard st.
Olsson, Chas.	8	Hull st.	Percy, Ernest	27	Marion rd.
Olsson, Fred A.	492	Common st.	Perino, Harry	39	Baker st.
Olsson, Jacob	79	Beech st.	Perino, Joe	5	A st.
O'Neil, Michael A.	24	Falmouth st.	Perino, Nicola	12	Baker st.
O'Neil, Thomas H. 2nd.	491	Belmont st.	Perkins, Wilfred D.	215	White st.
O'Neil, William		Pleasant st.	Perrault, James E,	21	Falmouth st.
O'Neill, Joseph S.	37	Goden st.	Perry, Joseph E.	59	Sycamore st.
Ordway, Walter M.	15	Exeter st.	Perry, Leon	263	Waverley st.
Orsett, Coy		Orchard st. ext.	Perry, Stanley R.	14	Marion st.
Oteri, Antonio	17	Grant av.	Peterson, Albert	19	Concord av.
Oteri, Gregorio	17	Grant av.	Peterson, John	69	Grove st.
Oteri, Harry R.	4	Sycamore st.	Phelps, Harry E.	64	David rd.
Otiro, Harry	39	Baker st.	Philbrick, Otis	489	Common st.
O'Toole, Peter	321	Concord av.	Pierce, Chas. W.	189	Lexington st.
Over, Chester H.	3	Oxford av.	Pierce, Harry W.	11	Whitcomb st.
Overlan, John J.	55	Maple st.	Pierpont, Frank	93	Beech st.
Packard, Dr. Frederic H.		Pleasant st.	Piper, Fred E. R.	42	Falmouth st.
Page, George A.	438	Trapelo rd.	Pisaturo, Carmine	20	Trowbridge st
Page, Maurice J.	5	Concord av.	Pitrone, Angelo	57	Baker st.
Palfrey, Charles E.	6	Thayer st.	Pittenger, Chas.	55	Berwick st.
Palmer, Benedict F.	67	Goden st.	Pliskin, David	85	Beech st.
Palmer, Louis	3	Spinney ter.	Pliskin, Solomon	85	Beech st.
Palmer, Matthew J.	67	Goden st.	Plunkett, A. J.		Payson rd.
Paone, Gaetano	15	Walnut st.	Plunkett, Richard	244	Brighton st.
Parisi, Anthony	48	Grant av.	Plunkett, William	244	Brighton st.
Park, O. J.	4	Worcester st.	Pollard, Adrian	17	Oxford av.
Parker, Horace	401	Concord av.	Pollock, Leyland W.	130	White st.
Parker, John N.	92	Beech st.	Pompino, Chas.	82	Beech st.
Parker, Percy C.	52	Burnham st.	Poole, Ava	386	Common st.
Parker, Torrance		Concord av.	Poole, William H.	386	Common st.
Parker, Urban	12	Davis rd.	Pooler, Howard E.		Pleasant st.
Parker, Urban J.	12	Davis rd.	Poor, Fred	35	Waverley st.
Parks, Edward A.	26	Brighton st.	Porter, Louis F.	813	Belmont st.
Parks, Edward E.	442	Common st.	Porter, William M.	33	Marlboro st.
Parks, Frank E.	63	School st.	Potter, Frank S.	10	Davis rd.
Parks, Fred H.	26	Brighton st.	Potter, William A.	403	Trapelo rd.
Parks, Geo. W.	622	Trapelo rd.	Pound, Roscoe	490	Pleasant st.
Parks, William A.	622	Trapelo rd.	Powell, John R.	574	Trapelo rd.
Parry, Chas. G.	58	Dartmouth st.	Powers, Frank L.	87	Grove st.
Parsons, Albert E.	48	Alma av.	Powers, John E.	57	Thomas st.
Parsons, Herbert E.	50	Grove st.	Powers, Leslie M.	3	Marion rd.
Pasley, William A.	9	Moraine st.	Powers, Richard M.	12	Oxford av.

NAME.	NO.	STREET.	NAME.	NO.	STREET.
Preble, Geo. E.	15	Lawndale st.	Reynolds, Joseph G. Jr.	33	Willow st.
Preble, Leverett L.	6	Worcester st.	Reynolds, J. L.	40	Falmouth st.
Prentice, Theodore J.	8	Cherry st.	Reynolds, Michael B.	22	Ericsson st.
Prentiss, Geo. A.		Prospect st.	Reynolds, Michael J.	6	Hull st.
Prentiss, John H.		Prospect st.	Reynolds, Percy I.	440A	Common st.
Prentiss, Joseph		Prospect st.	Reynolds, William	19	Marlboro st.
Prescott, Frank J.	47	Payson rd.	Rhynd, Robert M.	257	Waverley st.
Pressy, Rev. Edwin S.	53	School st.	Ricco, Antonio	54	Baker st.
Pressy, Sidney L.	53	School st.	Rich, Robert R.	56	Dartmouth st.
Preston, Frank S.	268	Common st.	Rich, Samuel T.	16	Ericsson st.
Preston, J. Stanley	431	Trapelo rd.	Richards, Earle R.	50	Oxford av.
Preston, Willian A.	431	Trapelo rd.	Richardson, James M.	468	School st.
Pretat, Charles J.	39	Marion rd.	Richardson, J. Herbert		Hill rd.
Price, Eden	334	Pleasant st.	Richardson, J. Howard		Huron av.
Price, Lewis V.	666	Pleasant st.	Richardson, William	268	Washington st
Priest, Charles M.		Church st. p'.	Richardson, William B.	62	White st.
Probert, Albert A.	58	Dartmouth st.	Richert, C. Henry	583	Belmont st.
Pugh, Willian J.	20	Exeter st.	Richmond, Harold E.	20	Hillside ter.
Puleio, Nunzio	9	A st.	Riley, Patrick	31	Brighton st.
Purington, George C.	54	Burnham st.	Ripley, Harry M.	113	White st.
Purrington, Oliver Rev.	27	Cedar rd.	Ripley, Leonard F.	113	White st.
Putnam, Walter A.		Clark st.	Ripley, Orville	189	White st.
Putney, George A.	21	Whitcomb st.	Robbins, Arthur G.	42	Oak st.
Quigley, Edward W.	60	Thomas st.	Robbins, Chandler	727	Pleasant st.
Quigley, Edward F.	56	Thomas st.	Robbins, Raymond L.	56	Berwick st.
Quigley, James	194	Waverley st.	Robbins, Samuel D.	727	Pleasant st.
Quigley, James A.	60	Thomas st.	Roberts, David R.	69	Grove st.
Quigley, Patrick	17	Woodland st.	Roberts, David R. Jr.	69	Grove st.
Quigley, Patrick	56	Thomas st.	Robertson, Duncan A.	111	Sycamore st.
Quinn, Mitchell	248	Mill st.	Robertson, Murdick	182	Concord av.
Quinn, Murray		Pleasant st.	Robinson, E. J.	115	Pine st.
Quinn, Theodore		Pleasant st.	Robinson, Edgar W.	18	Goden st.
Raddin, Thomas	90	Pine st.	Robinson, Edward K.		Kilburn rd.
Ramobln, Gene	34	Grant av.	Robinson, Geo. E.	130	Waverley st.
Rand, Earl P.		Wellington st.	Robinson, Guy H.	34	Goden st.
Randall, Tony	13	Underwood st.	Robinson, Jabez L.		Orchard st.
Ransom, Horace U.	27	Orchard st.	Robinson, Oliver C.	57	Burnham st.
Raymond, Warren S.	41	Waverley st.	Robinson, Roy L.	98	Trapelo rd.
Read, Elmer C.	71	Orchard st.	Robinson, Sumner B.	34	Goden st.
Reader, George	41	Unity av.	Robinson, Vernon C.	580	Trapelo rd.
Redding, Michael	76	Cross st.	Robinson, Walter H.	16	Exeter st.
Redding, Patrick	76	Cross st.	Robinson, William F.	59	Sycamore st.
Redfield, Irving L.	8	Agassiz av.	Rock, Harry	29	Harriet av.
Reed, Albert F.	214	White st.	Rockett, John W.	22	Ericsson st.
Reed, Albert H.	210	Payson rd.	Rockwell, Wallace L.	6	Springfield st.
Reed, Andrew F.	90	Somerset st.	Rold, Chas. H.	15	Vincent av.
Reed, Bryon W.	17	Oxford av.	Rold, Harry C.	153	Beech st.
Reed, Chas. C.	175	White st.	Rold, Irving E.	15	Vincent av.
Reed, Leslie B.	81	Concord av.	Rogers, Dr. Mark H.		Orchard st.
Reed, Thomas E.	701	Pleasant st.	Rogers, James F.	32	Grove st.
Reed, William J.	47	School st.	Rogers, Joseph	337	Concord av.
Reed, X. Allen	701	Pleasant st.	Rollins, Harold E.	51	Marion rd.
Reeves, F. H.	10	Holt st.	Rollins, William S.	61	Orchard st.
Reid, Peter M.	11	Harriet av.	Roper, Chas. H.	17	Falmouth st.
Reilly, Edward	16	Spring st.	Roper, John M.	58	Marlboro st.
Reilly, Matthew	16	Spring st.	Rose, Joseph	233	Common st.
Reilly, Russell G.	229	Belmont st.	Rose, Louis E.	171	Belmont st.
Remington, Charles E.	56	Oxford av.	Rose, Peter A.	12	Exeter st.
Restano, Rocky	9	B st.	Rose, William O.	14	Marlboro st.
Restuicco, Dominio		David rd.	Rosenberger, Fred B.	97	Oak av.
Restuccia, John	66	Hull st.	Roslund, John	65	Marlboro st.

ALPHABETICAL LIST OF POLLS.—*Con.*

NAME.	NO.	STREET.	NAME.	NO.	STREET.
Ross, Arthur		Pleasant st.	Scott, Frank A.	30	Blake st.
Ross, R. N.	24	Marion rd.	Scott, James P.	26	Cutter st.
Ross, Wilbert A.	220	White st.	Scotton, Alfred E.	30	Falmouth st.
Rotchford, James F.	29	Hawthorn st.	Scottron, Samuel J.	14	Thayer rd.
Rote, Charles C.	34	Falmouth st.	Schrader, Carl L.	58	Payson rd.
Rote, Donald I.	34	Falmouth st.	Scranton, Carl	37	Burnham st.
Rounsefell, Dr. Clifford G.	1075	Pleasant st.	Scribner, Fred W.	52	Agassiz av.
Rounsefelt, Guy P.	16	Cutter st.	Seaberg, Harry	64	Dartmouth st.
Rowe, Claude	248	Mill st.	Seaver, Robert	154	Mill st.
Rowley, Leonard W.		Townsend rd.	Seaverance, Leon M.	6	Townsend rd.
Runey, Leon C.	49	Fairmont st.	Secor, Henry B.	83	School st.
Russell, Clarence A.	42	Lexington st.	Sellers, Arthur	371	Concord av.
Russell, Elmer A.	50	Payson rd.	Sellers, William A.	371	Concord av.
Russell, George H.	352	Pleasant st.	Severance, Geo. A.	15	Whitcomb st.
Russell, Herbert H.	206	Lexington st.	Sexton, Geo. A.		Kilburn rd.
Russell, Ralph P.	18	Falmouth st.	Shaplaigh, William P.	15	Kilburn rd.
Ryan, C. Tracy	201	Lexington st.	Shaughnessy, Daniel R.	9	Maple st.
Ryan, Daniel	66	Spring st.	Shaughnessy, Eugene	9	Maple st.
Ryan, Dennis	670	Concord av.	Shaughnessy, John J.	341	Trapelo rd.
Ryan, Dennis	66	Spring st.	Shaughnessy, Patrick J.	28	Maple st.
Ryan, Edward T.	670	Concord av.	Shaughnessy, Thomas	9	Maple st.
Ryan, Jeremiah F.	130	Common st.	Shaw, Edward H.	215	Washington st
Ryan, John W.	102	Brighton st.	Shaw, Fred H.	275	Washington st
Ryan, Jos. J.	130	Common st.	Shaw, Walter J.	39	Marion rd.
Ryan, Lawrence M.	130	Common st.	Shea, John F.	107	Beech st.
Ryan, Michael J.	130	Common st.	Shean, Patrick H.	17	School st.
Ryan, Thomas	25	Baker st.	Shean, Patrick T.		Shean rd.
Ryan, Walter D.	201	Lexington st.	Shean, Patrick T. Jr.		Shean rd.
Sacro, John	24	Trowbridge st.	Shean, Thomas	46	Cottage st.
Sagie, Joseph	24	Trowbridge st.	Shedd, A. Lincoln	64	Waverley st.
Salviano, Vincenzo	106	Waverley st.	Shedd, Herman	70	Thomas st.
Sammet, Joseph		Pleasant st.	Sheehan, Daniel F.	91	Beech st.
Samuelson, Oscar		Pleasant st.	Sherburn, John R.	40	Lexington st.
Sandborg, F. W.	77	Marlboro st.	Sherman, Charles W.	16	Myrtle st.
Sanborn, C. Francis	63	Berwick st.	Sherman, Henry	62	Thomas st.
Sanderson, Frank L.	335	Trapelo rd.	Sherman, Herbert L.	27	Clover st.
Sanderson, George J.	42	Cottage st.	Sherman, Lee	94	Sycamore st.
Sanderson, Wm. M.	1028	Pleasant st.	Shible, Albert	14	Cross st.
Sanderson, Wm. M.	1028	Pleasant st.	Shipley, Chas. P.	228	Waverley st.
Sandiford, Chester L.	9	Goden st.	Shirley, James F.	52	Grove st.
Sandiford, Ernest	9	Goden st.	Silber, Isaac	24	Maple st.
Sands, Frank	211	Common st.	Silva, John P.	61	Grove st.
Sautagiato, Nino	64	Hull st.	Simm, Alva C.	614	Trapelo rd.
Sargent, Frank F.	80	Clark st.	Simm, Fred E.	16	Holt st.
Sargent, Geo. M. D.	548	Pleasant st.	Simm, Wilbert E.	574	Trapelo rd.
Sargent, James K. P.	80	Clark st.	Simm, William J.	580	Trapelo rd.
Sawyer, Fred S.	15	Stone rd.	Simonds, James O.	37	Somerset st.
Sayles, Dwight M.	20	Moore st.	Simonds, Otis	30	Somerset st.
Scaffo, Vincenzo	87	Hull st.	Simonds, Sidney L.	37	Somerset st.
Scanlon, Harold V.	4	Goden st.	Simpson, Albert		Pleasant st.
Scarfo, Tony	rear 343	Pleasant st.	Simpson, Hiram L.	92	Trapelo rd.
Scarfo, Salvatore	19	Grant av.	Sjolander, John O.	78	Oxford av.
Schaab, Philip A.	65	Fairview av.	Skahan, Edward F.	91	Grove st.
Schliephake, Robert H.	85	Beech st.	Skahan, John J.	23	Fairview av.
Schmuck, Bernard		Benjamin rd.	Skahan, John W.	74	Grove st.
Schultz, Rudulph	182	Waverley st.	Slade, Harold L.	7	Alexander av
Schutz, William C.	54	Marlboro st.	Slade, Walter H.	off	Common st.
Scinicariello, Tobia	39	Hawthorn st.	Slater, John T. H.	13	Sycamore st.
Scott, Chas. O.	340	Lake st.	Slayter, Henry S.	28	Pine st.
Scott, Chas. S.	91	Lexington st.	Sliney, David	319	Concord av.
Scott, Edward H.	53	Moraine st.	Sliney, Edward	63	Thomas st.

NAME.	NO.	STREET.	NAME.	NO.	STREET.
Sliney, John	267	Waverley st.	Stewart, Arthur M.	212	Payson rd.
Sliney, John	62	Thomas st.	Stewart, A. U.	10	Park rd.
Sliney, Michael	17	Ash st.	Stewart, John	95	Beech st.
Sliney, Thomas	11	Ash st.	Stewart, Thomas	337	Trapelo rd.
Small, Charles C.	149	Beech st.	Stiansen, Axel H.	2	Marion rd.
Small, Dr. Ernest W.	68	Leonard st.	Stockwell, Geo. P.	140	Beech st.
Smedile, Andrew	9	B st.	Stone, Arthur P.	613	Pleasant st.
Smidili, Peter	59	Grant av.	Stone, Chas. A.	49	Alma av.
Smith, Austin C.	25	Wilson av.	Stone, Fred	49	Alma av.
Smith, Chas. E.		Winter st.	Stone, Howard A.	26	Cedar rd.
Smith, Edward A.	13	Park rd.	Stone, Joseph C. R.	70	School st.
Smith, Fred A.	231	White st.	Stone, Joseph E.	21	Clover st.
Smith, Fred E.	31	Bartlett av.	Stone, Walter H.	162	Washington st
Smith, Fred L.	49	Cushing av.	Stonemetz, John C.	33	Willow st.
Smith, Geo. E.	93	School st.	Stover, Elroy S.	64	Berwick st.
Smith, Horace C.	566	Trapelo rd.	Stowe, Carle	158	White st.
Smith, Nelson J.	7	Davis rd.	Stowe, Clarence G.	23	Waverley st.
Smith, Owen J.	29	Marion rd.	Strange, Edgar	248	Mill st.
Smith, Patrick J.	65	Grove st.	Stratton, George	248	Mill st.
Smith, Thomas J.	70	Oxford av.	Strout, Vernon L.	150	Beech st.
Smith, William H.	57	Agassiz av.	Strum, Clarence E.	225	White st.
Smith, William J.	79	Walnut st.	Stuart Charles W.	101	Beech st.
Snow, Alfred J.	9	Agassiz av.	Stuart, Everett J.	101	Beech st.
Snow, Augustus W.	40	Church st.	Stuart, William A.	125	Waverley st.
Sorkin, Jacob	24	Maple st.	Stults, John V. N.	315	Belmont st.
Southard, Charles B.		Concord av.	Sullivan, Daniel	35	Cross st.
Sparrow, W. A.		David rd.	Sullivan, John	117	Belmont st.
Sparrow, Wendell H.	46	Waverley st.	Sullivan, John F.	127	Belmont st.
Spear, Alonzo P.	17	Falmouth st.	Sullivan, Simon	46	Chandler st.
Specht, Alden S.	26	Park rd.	Sullivan, Patrick	74	Waverley st.
Specht, K. E.	37	Grove st.	Sullivan, Stephen F.	489	Trapelo rd.
Spegio, Frank	29	Baker st.	Sullivan, William	off	Pleasant st.
Speiss, Dennis		Pleasant st.	Sutcliffe, Everett	120	Sycamore st.
Spidle, J. Lawrence	98	Sycamore st.	Suydam, Charles	18	Moore st.
Spinna, Joseph	35	Cross st.	Svenson, E.	77	Marlboro st.
Spinney, Edmund C.	98	Sycamore st.	Svensson, Lars A.	25	Marion rd.
Splaine, Richard H.	19	Exeter st.	Swaduski, Jake	308	Baker st.
Sprague, Willard, H.	111	Pine st.	Swain, Edward	560	Concord av.
Sprague, William	174	Lexington st.	Swain, Leonard	560	Concord av.
Stacey, Clifford L.	12	Sycamore st.	Swain, William C.	17	Oxford av.
Stackhouse, Hartley	347	Trapelo rd.	Swanson, Emil	729	Belmont st.
Stankhard, John J.	231	White st.	Swanson, Nils P.	164	Beech st.
Stanley, John D.	248	Mill st.	Swanson, Manfred	17	Park rd.
Staples, John L.	319	Brighton st.	Sweat, Augustus T.	97	School st.
Staples, Warren	319	Brighton st.	Sweeney, Maurice H.	17	Baker st.
Stearns, Edward H.	122	Brighton st.	Sweetmen, John	70	Somerset st.
Stearns, E. Truman	104	School st.	Symonds, Harold V.	17	Ridge rd.
Stearns, Harry C.	62	Sycamore st.	Syverson, S.	20	Marion rd.
Stearns, Milton S.	64	Goden st.	Taft, Roger B.	84	Goden st.
Stearns, Sherman	56	Marlboro st.	Talbot, Walter J.	171	Beech st.
Steele, Augustine J.	56	Dartmouth st.	Tapley, Albert A.	11	Springfield st.
Steeves, Everett W.	63	Berwick st.	Taylor, Albert B.	10	Falmouth st.
Sterritt, William W.	16	Ridge rd.	Taylor, Amos L.	117	School st.
Stevens, Chas. B.	10	Frederick st.	Taylor, Arthur	354	Lake st.
Stevens, Edward H.	40	Waverley st.	Taylor, Edwin P.	168	White st.
Stevens, Fred	16	Ericsson st.	Taylor, Frederick J.	9	Exeter st.
Stevens, Geo. W.	582	Pleasant st.	Taylor, Henry W.	12	Burnham st.
Stevens, Henry M.	40	Waverley st.	Taylor, James H.	15	Ash st.
Stevens, Herbert A.	38	Falmouth st.	Taylor, John	52	Waverley st.
Stevens, Hermon W.	30	Clover st.	Taylor, John	88	Bartlett av.
Stevens, Walter L. Jr	438	Trapelo rd.	Taylor, Walter D.	91	Beech st.

ALPHABETICAL LIST OF POLLS.—*Con.*

NAME.	NO.	STREET.	NAME.	NO.	STREET.
Taylor, William	52	Waverley st.	Upham, Thomas A.	35	Holt st.
Teed, William E.	20	Wilson av.	Valenti, Tony	59	Baker st.
Telford, William	24	Grant av.	VanDoren, J. Edward	50	Pine st.
Telker, Leon L.		Pleasant st.	VanWyck, Clarence B.	31	Willow st.
Temple, Edward H.	492	Common st.	Vaughan, F. W.	177	Belmont st.
Temple, Edward H. Jr.	35	Orchard st.	Venuti, John	9	Grant av.
Terrio, Simon H.	52	Marlboro st.	Vethas, Parvel	431	School St.
Terry, Orrin	70	White st.	Vickberg, Abel	145	Belmont st.
Thomas, Charles R.	741	Concord av.	Vigneau, Leo B.	11	Oak av.
Thomas, Chester R.	37	Holt st.	Vine, Franklin H.	32	Wilson av.
Thomas, Clifton G.	4	Bartlett rd.	Virchow, Albert G.	365	Trapelo rd.
Thomas, David L.	741	Concord av.	Virchow, Carl F.	365	Trapelo rd.
Thomas, William H.	37	Holt st.	Vollentine, Charles H.	26	Cushing av.
Thompson, Edward J.	22	Ridge rd.	Vollentine, Charles H. Jr.	26	Cushing av.
Thompson, Ernest H.	22	Ridge rd.	Vollentine, Thomas	26	Cushing av.
Thorndike, Leonidas M.	103	Sycamore st.	Waid, John F.	21	Marion rd.
Thulin, Walfred	22	Pine st.	Walcott, George P.	500	Pleasant st.
Thyne, John	76	Cross st.	Walcott, Oliver	76	Oxford av.
Tibeau, Peter	27	Underwood st.	Waldo, Clinton F.		Pleasant st.
Tiernay, Thomas J.	37	Grove st.	Waldo, William R.	76	Unity av.
Tierney, Nicholas W.		Chenery ter.	Waldon, Charles H.	641	Pleasant st.
Tilton, William	102	Brighton st.	Walker, Charles H.	63	Berwick st.
Tingley, Charles H.	51	Agassiz av.	Walker, James		Huron av.
Tippett, Thomas M.	163	Belmont st.	Walker, Lyman	24	Stone rd.
Tobin, Patrick F.	74	School st.	Walker, William H.	45	Willow st.
Tolland, Daniel	194	Waverley st.	Wall, William	24	Cross st.
Tompkins, Edward		Pleasant st.	Wallace, William	16	Thayer rd.
Toomey, Timothy F.	200	Waverley st.	Wallace, William O.	24	Maple st.
Towle, Herbert C.	47	Marion rd.	Wallace, William T.	24	Maple st.
Towne, Joseph L.	150	Beech st.	Walsh, Edward E.	81	Dartmouth st.
Tracy, John J.	263	Waverley st.	Walsh, Matthew J.	16	Cambridge st.
Tracy, Maurice L.	61	Waverley st.	Walsh, Michael	7	Maple ter.
Travaglio, Frank	11	Walnut st.	Walsh, William	7	Maple ter.
Tremplay, Edmund J.	5	Chestnut st.	Walton, Perry	33	Wellington av.
Trenholm, Charles E.		Townsend rd.	Ward, Arthur H.		Pleasant st.
Trew, John	5	Wilson av.	Ward, Ralph C.	35	Marion rd.
Tricone, Gregori	64	Hull st.	Ward, William H.		Pleasant st.
Tricone, Sebastin	4	Sycamore st.	Ware, Leslie A.	106	Grove st.
Troccoli, Achli	426	Trapelo rd.	Warner, Charles B.		Pleasant st.
Trowbridge, Merle E.	19	Moraine st.	Warren, Charles	112	Waverley st.
Trowbridge, William C.	19	Moraine st.	Warren, Orvis A.	100	White st.
Troy, John E.	586	Trapelo rd.	Warwick, Geo. W.	399	Belmont st.
Troy, Martin	586	Trapelo rd.	Washburn, Dexter	211	Common st.
True, Ross	37	Wilson av.	Waterbury, William	6	Agassiz av.
Tucker, Edward P.	548	Trapelo rd.	Waterbury, William F.	5	Marion rd.
Tucker, George M.	12	Blake st.	Wateroff, Geo. J.		Pleasant st.
Tucker, Warren W.	190	Lexington st.	Watson, Charles H.	60	Clark st.
Tufts, Royal G.	26	Marion rd.	Webber, Arthur M.	66	Leonard st.
Tukey, Frederick J.	92	Sycamore st.	Webber, Walter L.	114	White st.
Turk, Frank W.	163	Belmont st.	Webster, C. W.	23	Oak av.
Turk, Joseph M.	9	Marlboro st.	Webster, Henry E.	75	Waverley st.
Tuttle, G. Raymond	17	Ridge rd.	Webster, John	94	Sycamore st.
Tuttle, Dr. Geo. T.		Pleasant st.	Webster, Daniel P.	75	Waverley st.
Tuttle, Henry E.	24	Oak st.	Weeks, Bedford H.	79	Marlboro st.
Twomey, George H.	73	Grove st.	Weeks, Cyrus	37	Marlboro st.
Underhill, Edward E.	20	Marlboro st.	Weeks, Harold E.	79	Marlboro st.
Underhill, Henry	43	Maple st.	Weiler, Ernest C.	55	Sycamore st.
Underwood, Henry O.	100	Common st.	Wellington, C. Oliver	off	Concord av.
Underwood, Loring	90	Common st.	Wellington, William W.	631	Pleasant st.
Underwood, William J.	50	Common st.	Wellman, Geo. F.	17	Lawndale st.
Underwood, W. Lyman	50	Common st.	Wellman, Walter F.	17	Lawndale st.

Alphabetical List of Polls.—*Con.*

Name.	No.	Street.	Name.	No.	Street.
Wells, Frederic Lyman		Pleasant st.	Wildes, Charles H.	125	Waverley st.
Wells, Jeremiah B.	249	Waverley st.	Wiley, Arthur M.	47	Marion rd.
Wellsman, George A.	439	Trapelo rd.	Willard, Frank H.	130	Waverley st.
Wellsman, J. C.	7	Moraine st.	Williams, Bertrand P.		Hill rd.
Wellsman, J. Fred	439	Trapelo rd.	Williams, George A.	435	Trapelo rd.
Wendell, Charles B.	43	Oak av.	Williams, Ralph E.		Hill rd.
Wentworth, Miles S.	72	Payson rd.	Williams, Salibury H.	435	Trapelo rd.
Wentzel, Philip	430	Trapelo rd.	Willis, John		Pleasant st.
Werge, John A.	13	Marion rd.	Willison, Elmer C.	92	Payson rd.
Westby, Peter	57	Marlboro st.	Willison, Howard W.	92	Payson rd.
Westcott, James H.	101	Beech st.	Williston, Samuel	577	Belmont st.
Westhaver, David	16	Marlboro st.	Wilson, Frank	87	Walnut st.
Westland, Gustaf	3	Marion rd.	Wilson, George L.	90	School st.
Weston, Ernest	35	Falmouth st.	Wilson, John	119	Lexington st.
Weston, Geo. M.	159	Brighton st.	Wilson, J. W.	13	Maple ter.
Weston, Geo. W.		Waverley st.	Wilson, Thomas	87	Walnut st.
Weston, Louis F.	35	Falmouth st.	Winship, Harry H.	27	Francis st.
Weston, Wellis P.	159	Brighton st.	Winslow, Everett M.	2	Thayer rd.
Westphal, August	8	Agassiz av.	Wisdom, Arthur A.		Payson rd.
Weymouth, Guy	10	Marlboro st.	Wolff, Louis J.	578	Trapelo rd.
Whalen, Andrew J.	30	Trowbridge st.	Wood, Dana M.	22	Myrtle st.
Whalen, Michael J.	30	Trowbridge st.	Wood, George D.	18	Marion rd.
Whalen, William	off	Pleasant st.	Wood, George E.		Pleasant st.
Wheeler, Daniel H.		Pleasant st.	Wood, Henry B.	35	Myrtle st.
Wheeler, Frank E.	35	Pine st.	Wood, Isaac P.	375	School st.
Whelan, James F.	184	Concord av.	Wood, James F.	28	Pine st.
Whipple, Clarence M.		Benjamin rd.	Woodberry, Robert C.	90	Somerset st.
White, Clarence S.	97	Somerset st.	Woodin, George R.	23	Oak st.
White, D. Winthrop	37	Marlboro st.	Woods, Henry W.	343	Pleasant st.
White, Edward	306	Washington st.	Woods, Herbert S.	9	Hull st.
White, Edward K.	172	Beech st.	Woods, William M.	83	Lexington st.
White, Frank S.	84	Payson rd.	Woolfrey, Gilbert	9	Slade st.
White, Herbert	371	Concord av	Woolfrey, George	9	Slade st.
White, Herbert M.	84	Payson rd.	Worcester, Edwin G.	20	Oak st.
White, Patrick	19	Concord av.	Wright, George C.		Chestnut st.
Whitehill, Walter M.	15	Chandler st.	Wright, Willis F.	113	White st.
Whiting, Hebert E.	1032	Pleasant st.	Yantosca, Murray		Alexander av.
Whiting, John G.	1032	Pleasant st.	Young, Archibald F. R.	74	Agassiz av.
Whiting, Thomas H.	1032	Pleasant st.	Young, Frank E.		Church st. pl.
Whitney, Dr. Ray Lester	127	Mill st.	Young, George U.	10	Cambridge st.
Whitney, William R.		Church st. pl.	Young, Henry	220	White st.
Whittemore, Casper M.	12	Marion rd.	Young, Herbert	343	Waverley st.
Whittemore, Earl C.	47	Maple st.	Young, Ulysses S.	132	White st.
Wien, Paul A.	28	Bartlett av.	Zelefiski, Tony	308	Brighton st.
Wilcocks John	17	Myrtle st.	Zona, John	55	Baker st.
Wilcomb, Charles L.	20	Moraine st.